Wrestling
with
Tradition

D1527700

Wrestling
with
Tradition

Dale Stopperan

For my wonderful, supportive wife, our kids, and all my wrestlers.

I want to thank my wife, Kris, and my daughters for giving up years of winter Saturdays supporting my passion and my wrestling teams. I thank my sons for choosing to wrestle for me and for the hours we spent together. There is a deep appreciation for my fellow coaches and all the young men and ladies that wrestled for me. You all inspired me to write this book. A special thank you to my brothers who excelled in the sport of wrestling and motivated me to complete and publish "Wrestling with Tradition."

CHAPTER 1
CRESCO

The lights glowed over the tennis court after sunset in this small northeast Iowa town, but no one played tennis. Voices rang out in the night air from outside the fenced area. "Get him! Get him! Cross face! Don't let him in on your leg, ahh! Turn the corner! Sprawl!" A chorus of "oooooh..." swelled, followed by, "Two, two, two!" Finally, a ripple of laughter and a couple of claps. Someone yelled, "I'm next!"

On this typical Iowa warm and too humid summer night, bicycles were lined up in a row, leaning against the outside of the Kessel Park tennis court fence. The collection included a variety of banana seats, butterfly handlebars, fat tires, and sissy bars, giving the appearance of having been pieced together in someone's garage. Swimsuits rolled up in towels were wedged in the crossbar of many bikes, while baseball gloves looped through and hung down from many handlebars.

Formed off the fence was a semi-circle of six

or seven cars and pickups, establishing a mini-arena area where the tennis court's lights highlighted two boys squaring off on the grass in the center. An apparent pecking order for observing the battle developed. The older high school kids sat on their car hoods or on the dropped tailgates of their pickups, which they backed into the edge of the circle. Some nights a tractor or two might be found parked on the limestone gravel drive. The junior high school-aged kids sat on the ground watching the action but hoped to be invited up to a tailgate. A few girls hung out with their boyfriends, just as interested in the action as the guys, and were surprisingly willing to shout out words of encouragement, triumph, or even disgust if the contestants were not mixing it up enough.

With sweat glistening off their bodies, two shirtless teens confronted each other in the middle of the make-shift ring. An unhooked strap from the older boy's dark blue well-worn coveralls hung down behind him. Beneath the tailgate of his family's Ford F-100 pickup laid his t-shirt, dusty boots, and socks. He felt the dirt grime between his toes as he stood barefooted, leaning forward over his front leg. An older spectator made fun of his 'farmer's tan,' comparing his white chest and shoulders to his bronze arms and face. Tan lines materialized around his neck and biceps, including his "WWB" or "white-wall band" on his forehead, where a distinct white-to-tan line developed where

10

a baseball cap protected his head from the sun.

"Show us your legs!"

"God no, we'll all go blind!"

A wave of laughter sounded but did not last because all the farm boys wore the same tans. It represented a symbol of farm pride resulting from hard work in the sun all day long. Light t-shirts with denim jeans or coveralls provided protection from the sun and daily bumps, bruises, and scrapes resulting from working in the fields and with livestock on the farms. Lately, the farmers baled hay from daybreak to sunset to stock up winter feed for their livestock, storing it in the haymows in their barns' top level. Many town kids took advantage of baling hay's labor opportunity to put additional cash in their pockets.

The opposing foe, a "townie" in clean blue gym shorts outlined in white, wore new white Adidas tennis shoes with three blue stripes on each side that matched the two stripes at the top of his calf-high white athletic socks. His blonde locks, quite long compared to the farm boys, parted in the middle and hung over the top of his ears. The back of his hair touched the collar of his red, white, and blue Chicago Cubs t-shirt.

He had jumped up and volunteered to be next but rapidly became intimidated by both his opponent and being the focus of attention. The swish sound of the opening of beer cans echoed out as the two boys slap hands signaling 'let's go' and

11

someone yelled, "Get him!"

In the summer on the grass and dirt, Wrestling Iowa style, precisely Cresco Iowa style, brings wrestlers together in the park to sharpen their skills and have some fun. The farm and small-town boys naturally develop their strength and balance from their hard work and long days, fostering determination and fearlessness, which came with completing chores necessary for survival. Each family member pulled their weight, and if they did not, there would be consequences. This work ethic's expectations initiated as soon as they were big enough to pick up a bucket.

Bing Natvig stepped into his frightened volunteer, reached across with an over-hook on his foe's right arm and an under-hook beneath his left armpit. Bing rolled his waist underneath and threw a brutal hip toss. The younger kid's feet flew eight feet in the air as he sailed across Bing's hips. The air rushed out as the teen landed on his back with a loud thud. He gasped for air as Bing landed directly on top of his chest. He heard a unison of "ouch" from the assembly of on-lookers. Out of a bit of compassion, Bing let him go immediately but left the enormous notion of intimidation. The youngster crawled over to his friends on his hands and knees, felt like throwing up, and prayed he would not cry. His buddies grimaced, thankful for being on the sidelines.

The Cresco version of 'King of the Hill' meant

the first grappler to get a takedown remained the winner or king and stayed in the center to take on the next competitor. On a usual night, Bing took down five or six participants before volunteering to step out to give others a chance. Bing moved back to the center, slightly leaning forward with his hands on his knees, waiting for his next victim.

Bing did not wait long. The newcomer had already stripped his t-shirt and actively removed his rubber barn boots, exposing his brown feet callused from not wearing socks. Charlie brought him to the park on Friday nights for most of the summer. "Let's go, spic," someone said. No one in the crowd second-guessed the statement or even thought of it being offensive or racist.

With his oversized Wrangler blue jeans, frayed at the bottom and cinched up by a green army surplus belt, the skinny shirtless Hispanic kid hustled out and faced Bing. The brown-skinned teen had yet to take an offensive shot throughout the summer. He displayed precise technique, and the group admired his defensive skills and his exceptional ability to counter for takedowns. Where he picked up his experience remained a mystery even to Charlie.

The duel began as the warriors shook hands. Bing reached up to tie up around the neck of his foe, and to his surprise, and everyone around the circle, the Hispanic lowered himself underneath Bing's extended arm, stepped under, and drove to a

13

double leg takedown by wrapping both arms around Bing's upper legs. He elevated Bing and dropped him on his hip to the grass and dirt. Bing immediately scrambled up, rotated, cross-faced him, and pushed him away.

A voice shrieked, "Two!"

"Dude, did you see that? The greaser got him!"

"Bingo, the Mexican took ya down."

"How's it feel to get taken down by a spic?"

Bing did not display any signs of having given up a takedown and continued to wrestle. Furious, he jammed the kid with both hands in the core of his chest and shoved him up against the tennis court fence. The Hispanic boy did not react and just relaxed.

"That's enough, Bingo," Drew called out. "Beaner got you. Let it go! Now that's a great shot."

The title of king or best wrestler on the team belonged to Bing Natvig. However, the title of best athlete Cresco High School ever produced belonged to Drew Parker. Bing peered over at Drew with half of a smirk and a nod, finally acknowledging the takedown. Drew's comment not only gave the new kid the takedown but unintentionally gave him a nickname meant to be kinder than the more derogatory names he heard. The cluster of teenagers picked up on it, and, for the first time all summer, guys talked to the new kid instead of about him.

"Nice shot, Beaner!"

"Way to go, Beaner!"

Bing released Beaner off the fence and put his hand out. "You're pretty good, Beaner."

Beaner, though unsure of his acceptance and his new nickname, slapped a five on Bing's hand, "Gracias."

A puzzled expression crossed Bing's face as Charlie boomed, "Geez, Bingo, it means 'thank you' in Spanish! Even I know that." His remarks brought a few chuckles from the teenagers because Charlie was not renowned for his academic aspirations.

Suddenly someone whispered loudly, "Coach is coming!" The boys with beers scampered around to hide their stash.

Tom Kilmer and his wife, Lori, jogged up the brownish-yellow limestone path from the street. Periodically throughout the summer, Tom stopped by to check on his wrestlers, engaging the kids in conversations to build up their self-esteem and to develop rapport with each of them.

The mile and a quarter route from their house took them past the clinic to the south side of Kessel Park. They jogged alongside the row of twelve ash trees the city planted three years earlier to replace the row of sixty-foot tall elm trees sadly chain-sawed down and removed, with over forty other elm trees around the town affected by Dutch elm disease. The glow at the other end of the park defined their destination. As the twosome came out

15

of the shadows into the tennis court lights at the circle's edge, Beaner moved to the hub.

"Looking good tonight, Mrs. Coach!" a male voice announced from one of the pickup truck tailgates. A sound of a slap connecting on the side of a face pierced the night air. "Hey, what the heck was that for?"

A scolding girl's squeaky voice proclaimed, "You don't talk to Mrs. Kilmer that way!"

"Thank you, Beverly," Lori Kilmer, hiding the fact the comment flattered her, smiled at Beverly.

Lori was a beautiful, petite but curvy woman, and on this hot, humid summer evening, she dressed in her red running shorts, a white tank top, and low-cut blue Nike running shoes with the new Swoosh logo. She felt the bead of sweat, caused more likely by the high humidity than from the workout, roll from her scalp onto her forehead and reached up, and wiped it aside. Nearly thirty years old, she projected a pride of fitness, particularly the definition in her biceps and calf muscles and her consciousness of a healthy lifestyle. The youthful couple exercised together daily during the summer months. Unlike the 'meat and potatoes' most mid-westerners claimed with enthusiasm, they appreciated a diet including plenty of fresh fruits and vegetables.

She re-tied her long blonde ponytail and began walking around the perimeter. Like a second mother, especially during the wrestling season, Lori acknowledged many of the teens by name and asked about their summers and families. The group called her 'Mrs. Coach' out of endearment and out of respect for her husband.

Tom Kilmer sat down on the nearest tailgate next to Drew, who slid over to give him room. The young coach gave Drew a friendly punch on the upper arm, and Drew returned the gesture. Wearing his well-worn Moorhead State College Wrestling 1964 NIAA National Champions t-shirt along with his blue Cresco Wrestling gym shorts, he called out to the bunch, "Hey, guys! How we doing tonight?"

Composing mental notes, Tom scanned the collection of school kids, not so much to see who was there, but more about who was not. He was careful not to look too closely, as he had a high suspicion a few beers were probably around the circle. Farm families, especially the ones of German and Irish heritage, often quenched a thirst with a beer in celebration of a hard day's work on a hot hay baling day, and a few of those beers might have come to town.

"Doing good, coach."

"Thanks for coming by."

"Hey, you just missed an unbelievable one!"

The last statement caught his attention as he immediately turned to Drew and raised his eyebrows. Drew nodded towards the lean Mexican kid who stood in the core of the circle. "Beaner, there, just took Bing down."

17

Coach tilted his head sideways and smiled in disbelief. "Really?"

He leaned forward past Drew, attempting to make eye contact with Bing. Usually, Bingo would be one of the first to interact by greeting the coach. Out of embarrassment for getting taken down, Bing intentionally avoided Tom by turning towards the girl sitting next to him. She appeared to be disinterested. Coach muttered, "Well, I'll be damned," primarily to himself, responding to Bing's reluctance to engage with him, which validated the fact someone took him down. Tom focused his attention to the middle of the ring, where he watched the black-haired, brown-skinned Mexican with a noticeable mustache easily counter his fresh competitor's single-leg attack and spin around for a takedown. Coach looked again at Drew, who raised his eyebrows and bobbed his head up and down.

Without pausing for an answer, Coach mumbled, "Where did he come from? What's he weigh? Ya know, he might fit in, but we will have to wait to see if he comes to school or is even here during the wrestling season. Gotta go."

Tom leaped off the truck tailgate and yelled out. "Don't be doin' anything stupid. Be good! Get it?"

"Got it!" came the group response.

As the Kilmers jogged off, they heard, "Ya sure, you betcha, Coach. We're ALWAYS good!" The group erupted in laughter.

18

CHAPTER 2
COACH

Tom Kilmer grew up in Anoka, Minnesota, where his parents owned the Anoka Hardware & Bait and Tackle Store on Ferry Street less than half a mile north of where the Rum River empties into the Mississippi River. The building had an old wooden plank loading dock on its backside for alley access and deliveries, while the front of the store looked over Ferry Street at the Rum River. Blue with red diamonds linoleum covered the three extended aisles leading to the back check-out counter and its brown push-button National cash register. Tools and bins of nails, nuts, bolts, and screws occupied one outer aisle while fishing poles, fishing gear, and an old single-door refrigerator with the words "Live Bait" spray-painted in red on the front, lined the opposite aisle. The center aisle contained general hardware and seasonal supplies.

A repair shop for bicycles and fishing gear occupied the rear of the store, with an entrance off the loading dock. A yellow drop leaf kitchen table with its sides folded down and three stools with matching yellow vinyl-covered seats mended with duct tape sat adjacent to the oil burner heater at the far end of the repair shop. A red Coca-Cola bottle top-loading vending machine anchored the corner on the other side of the table. During the winter months, the table became a gathering spot for locals and customers to 'chew the fat.' As a young teenager, Tom learned to drink coffee at this table.

The whole family helped with the business. Being a wizard with bookkeeping, his mother had the responsibility for the store's finances and payroll. Sales came naturally for his father. He loved to share his knowledge and felt it as a duty to make sure customers had the right tools and all the information they needed. His reputation for his fishing knowledge brought customers into the store from throughout the region, including the greater Twin Cities area.

When the school bell would ring at the end of the day, the Kilmer kids would head to the store to do their share by sweeping the floors and sidewalks, taking out the garbage, and dusting and reorganizing shelves. Saturday mornings, the youngsters, wearing white three-pocket canvas work aprons with Anoka Hardware printed in maroon on the chest, stocked inventory by moving it from storage in the basement to the store floor. As they grew older, they helped on the sales floor and in the repair shop. Tom's school buddies stopped by the store now and then, teased him about his apron, and usually stayed around to have a Coke in the back room. Coming in with their parents, the girls told him how cute he looked in his work apron. Tom's face turned red in embarrassment.

Tom's dad educated his children about the store's products, their purposes, and how to share the information with customers. With every lesson, he said, "Get it?" If the kids understood, they replied, "Got it!" He taught his children how to respect and treat customers by telling his kids, "Remember people are more important than the work. Get it?"

"Got it!"

The community respected him for his integrity in running his business and respected him for how he raised his family. His parents closed the hardware store on Sundays to attend church services at the oldest and largest Lutheran Church in Anoka. Tom's great grandfather immigrated from Sweden and helped construct the original Zion Lutheran Church building.

It was not unusual for the home telephone to ring in the Kilmer house in the evening hours or on a Sunday afternoon, and their father politely headed to the store and took care of them. He carved out family time, teaching his children how to fish for smallmouth and largemouth bass, northern

21

pike, walleye, and trout. They fished nearby Crooked Lake and the Rum and Mississippi Rivers. Trolling for northern pike and lake trout in the Boundary Waters in up-state Minnesota embodied their summer vacations. Their winters included ice fishing for walleye in Lake Mille Lacs.

Tom knew every item and its spot on the shelves as a grade-schooler and became competent with building tools and building supplies before being old enough to get a driver's license. Like his father, Tom developed a passion for the fishing department.

The day Rocky Gwinn, the Anoka High School wrestling coach, walked in the store to get a new fishing pole transformed his life. The conversation between Rocky, Tom's dad, and twelve-year-old Tom turned from fishing to wrestling. Rocky described the sport's physical aspect and how fishing helped him develop his mental fortitude as a wrestler. Just like fishing, a wrestler competes by himself with no one else to blame for mistakes. Fishing taught him to study his opponent, to never be bothered by the score, and to show up when others would not, no matter the adversity.

Responding to Coach Gwinn's encouragement, Tom joined the junior high school wrestling squad and found he valued the physicality of the sport and relished his success. In high school, Tom and Rocky resumed their relationship surrounding wrestling and fishing. He worked extremely hard for Rocky, taking home a fourth-place medal from the state meet his senior year. Even though Tom considered himself an average student academically, Rocky encouraged him to go to college and become a teacher.

"I watch you work with our younger wrestlers. Like all good fishermen, you have the patience of Job. You are a fine teacher, Tom. Just find your passion. Maybe it is in education, and maybe someday you will come back and take over for me." Rocky grinned. "Whatever you choose to do, give it all you got. As I have heard your father say, get it?"

"Got it."

Tom had never thought of becoming a teacher. He figured he would take over the hardware store. But his mentor's words inspired him, so he joined his high school girlfriend at Moorhead State College across the Red River from Fargo, North Dakota. Halfway through the first quarter of the school year, his girlfriend dumped him for an upperclassman. It also may have been due to Tom spending his free time on a new challenge of fishing the 'Big Red' for channel catfish. Either way, Tom moved on and swiftly adapted to a college student's needs with his classes and work-study schedule, developing into an excellent student.

Tom's roommate wrestled for the University of Pittsburgh, but when he ended up on

23

academic probation, he decided to transfer to Moorhead State to wrestle for the Dragons. About the time Tom's girlfriend ditched him, his roommate, needing an additional work-out partner and knowing Tom wrestled in high school, convinced Tom to try out for the college's wrestling team. It did not take Tom long before realizing his wrestling abilities were nowhere near the same level as the recruits in the wrestling room.

Still, he dedicated himself to the physical aspects, and he advanced in his technical skills. His coaches and teammates appreciated his work ethic and camaraderie and snickered when Tom described college wrestling as his new girlfriend. Though he never cracked the varsity line-up, he stayed in top physical shape and seized the opportunity to wrestle in a couple of open tournaments each year. Tom remained in the wrestling program for three years and completed his collegiate wrestling career with seven wins and five losses. After his junior year, he ended his collegiate wrestling commitment to do his student teaching.

Fortunately, his student teaching experience at Moorhead High School offered the opportunity to help coach the high school wrestling team. Tom enjoyed teaching, but he treasured coaching. The coaching experience revealed to Tom the influence he had on his student-athletes' future under his tutelage. Continually thankful for his parents' love, support, and guidance, but for the first time, Tom began to realize the impact his high school coach had on him and how Rocky had influenced his life. The opportunity now laid in front of him to do the same for others.

As a coach, he would help wrestlers improve their wrestling skills and become more successful. He now understood how to use the sport of wrestling to help young men develop character traits of perseverance, self-control, dedication, and integrity. Although he associated his personal growth with his coaches, more important to him was the inspiration provided by his father as a role model and his father's guiding conversations, significantly when they went fishing. Tom finally understood that the life lessons he learned from his two favorite fishermen built his character. He now held the responsibility to pass those lessons on as a segment of his teaching and coaching philosophy.

He honed his skills during his teaching practicum, becoming exceptionally talented at both teaching and coaching. He could hardly wait to share what happened each day with his new girlfriend, Lori. He fell in love with her two and a half years earlier when she was dressed in corduroy overalls, swinging a hammer, and using a circular saw.

Tom's first teaching position, a health and physical education teacher at Cooper High School in northwest Minneapolis, included the assistant

25

wrestling coach position. Lori learned about 'cutting weight' and became an element of her husband's program by teaching his wrestlers the healthy ways for athletes to diet and lose weight.

Cooper High School won two Minnesota state wrestling team championships during Tom's tenure as an assistant coach. Tom took on more and more responsibilities each season, and six years later, he began searching for a head coaching position. He initially limited his search to the area around his familiar fishing holes in southern and central Minnesota. It took a phone call from his wrestling friend and former college roommate coaching in Austin, Minnesota, to spur Tom to apply for the teaching and coaching position in Cresco. The Cresco School Board hired Tom to teach physical education and steer the Spartan Wrestling program in the fall of 1971.

CHAPTER 3

MRS. COACH

Lori loved growing up on a Minnesota farm sixty miles west of Minneapolis near Litchfield, Minnesota. During World War II, her father served in the Army Air Corps' 316th Troop Carrier Group as a mechanic on a C-47 aircraft. Inducted into the army at nearby Fort Snelling, his basic training took place in Jefferson Barracks in Missouri. At the end of basics, with an unusual four-day pass, he had just enough time to travel home and marry his high school sweetheart before reporting to Sheppard Field in Texas for his specialized training and his departure to Europe.

Upon his discharge at the end of the war, Lori nearly two years old, he returned to Litchfield and helped with the family farm. A few years later, when her grandparents retired to town, Lori's father moved his family, which now included two younger brothers, to the farm, taking over the operation. Like most farm kids, Lori worked as hard as every other member of the family. Besides teaching her to farm and raise livestock, Lori's father did not hesitate in helping Lori develop her carpentry and mechanics abilities repairing most buildings, fences, or equipment on the farm. At the time, most people, even farmers, considered these skills reserved for the males of the family.

As proud of her father as she was, her mother served as her role model. Her father always pointed to his wife and told Lori, "If you grow up like your mom, loving God, and workin' hard, you'll be all right."

Though her father taught her farm skills, Lori learned the importance of her mother's tenacity and perseverance. Her mother believed in hard work, extensive days and acted as the morning alarm clock with what she called the 'morning announcements.'

Waking up to the sounds of "Wakey! Wakey! Eggs and Bakey!" "Time to go a Dancing!" "Day's a Wastin'!" or "A job begun is a job half done!" caused a repercussion of moans from the upstairs bedrooms. She then began shouting out a list of tasks for the day such as fixing fence, baling hay, chopping firewood, or painting the barn, concluding with a robust, drawn-out "AND"... "WE got breakfast in ten!" or "WE got SCHOOL today!"

Thinking fondly back about her mom's morning ritual, Lori remembers more than once, lying in bed, pulling her pillow over the top of her head to muffle the annoying voice of her mother waking them. The kids reminisced about one particular morning on the heels of an extremely long hard day of work on the farm. The then teenagers did not respond to the usual 5:30 call out, so, standing at the bottom of the stairway, their mother belted out a loud rendition of 'A Mighty Fortress is Our God.'

"My Goodness, Mother, enough is enough! We're up!"

"Good! It would be a terrible thing to see my children not standing for the Lord." They did not think it was funny at the time, but they prized the story as adults.

During his Army Air Corps experiences, Lori's father recognized that promotions and assignments were based not only on hard work but awarded for attaining additional training. He shared this with his wife, and they mutually recognized education as the key to success for the benefit of their children's future, and encouraging their children in school and pointing them to college became a priority.

At Moorhead State College, the female coed met an aspiring wrestler named Tom Kilmer while doing their work-study in the maintenance department. Tom tells how they were on a work crew together, on the far side of the campus, repairing a college storage barn, and saw Lori handling the circular saw. He says he fell in love with her right then and there, but it took him nearly three months to ask her out.

Lori always reminds him, he didn't initiate the first date. With Tom's roommate's help, Lori discovered his fishing spot on the Red River and, with borrowed fishing gear, nonchalantly showed up on the river bank one Saturday morning. Acting as if running into him was purely accidental, she contrived a fishing date out of him. Standing on the river's edge during their next outing, Lori finally confessed, "I'm ready to go home. I hate fishing! I just wanted you to ask me out."

"Oh, I knew you weren't a fisherman the first day you came out on the river. You don't catch catfish with a walleye lure." Tom sheepishly looked down. "I love hanging out with you, so I didn't say anything. How about a real date. I don't have a lot of money but maybe a pizza tonight?"

Acting angry, Lori playfully slapped his upper arm with the back of her hand, "Only if you promise not to ever, ever take me fishing again!"

"Deal!" He reached out to shake her hand to seal the agreement, but Lori stepped forward past his extended hand, grabbed both his shoulders, and kissed him. Although caught off guard, Tom promptly responded by returning her kiss and wrapped both arms around her waist.

Growing up as a hockey fanatic with her father, Lori took a while, but she slowly became a knowledgeable wrestling fan dating Tom for the next three years. In the fall of their senior year, Tom drug Lori along with him as he went fishing out on the edge of the Red River at the spot they first kissed. Reluctantly, Lori went along, complaining the entire way. As they walked along the riverbank, Tom carried his fishing pole, and Lori carried his creel. She continued to rant about how she had told him that she would never go fishing again. Tom ignored her comments as he stepped to the river's edge, examined the river's flow, and asked Lori to get his new fishing lure out of his creel. Lori kept complaining as she obliged him, found the new plastic case, and opened it. Suddenly she froze and became utterly silent. On the foam inside the case, Lori found a diamond engagement ring. As Tom nonchalantly threw out a cast, he asked, "Do you think I can catch anything with that?"

The next spring, the loving couple graduated, married, and settled in north Minneapolis. Tom began his teaching career, and Lori became a social worker for the State of Minnesota.

Lori's dream of raising children in a small town became part of the enticement of Cresco. She especially looked forward to living again in a small farming town where she could be involved in community and church activities. She secured a social worker position similar to her work in Minneapolis, covering much of northeast Iowa. They leased a beautiful cottage-style brick rental on the north side of town. The steeply pitched roof design with gingerbread trim, the window boxes, the round top front door, the hardwood floors, and the arched doorways were perfect. The landlord mentioned to them his interest in selling the home to them in the future. The discussion of purchasing the home and starting a family brought smiles to Tom's and Lori's faces, but both knew, though they never spoke of it, the upcoming wrestling season's success determined their fate in settling down in Cresco. Until then, the odd mixture of wrestlers, each with their unique personalities and issues, substituted as their family.

When they moved to Cresco the summer before school began in 1971, Tom set up a fundraiser involving clearing rocks from a farm field of his new landlord, a wrestling booster. This pasture of original prairie grass had never before been plowed under. The owner paid the team to walk the fourteen-acre field, dig out rocks, throw them on a hay wagon pulled by a tractor to get them off the field. Eighteen of his wrestlers showed up to help. When Lori climbed up on the John Deere to pull the hay wagon, they all looked at her and each other in disbelief. Upon arriving at Tom and Lori's home at the end of the day for a barbeque, the wrestlers kept ranting about the unexpected tractor driver. Lori said nothing and just beamed.

At tournaments, she arrived early with a cooler of food and a couple of decks of playing cards in her purse. When weigh-ins were completed, the grapplers chugged downed water or fruit juice and ate the food they each packed consisting of sandwiches and lots of junk food, including candy bars, cream-filled long-johns from the Cresco Bakery, and other store-bought snacks they shared. Lori's red and silver metal cooler contained apples, grapes, cheese, and homemade trail mix. She diligently circulated among the troops in an attempt to make the wrestlers eat more nutritionally.

During the three or four hours of downtime in the gym before the beginning of a tournament, some guys attempted to sleep on the wrestling mats while others tried to kill time by playing cards. 'Speed' became Lori's favorite card game to play with them, and she loved the thrill of beating them. "Ha! Gotch ya!" rang out, followed by her high-pitched laughter in the moments of victory.

More than just playing cards, Lori built strong relationships with her husband's athletes as they interacted during the card games. Reflecting aloud, they shared their personal stories and feelings, something that seldom happened for most of these young men. Although doing so was not thought to be a manly attribute, they 'spilled their guts' about their lives, including girlfriends, family dynamics, and school issues while playing cards with Mrs. Coach. Unintentionally and without being prompted, she was amazed by what the boys shared with her. Some of it nearly brought her to tears. With her social worker expertise, she did her best to

33

advise without judging them. They learned to trust Mrs. Coach and, in their ways, loved her.

In the summertime, the Kilmers hosted two or three picnics for the grapplers and their families. Tom knew in Cresco, Iowa, wrestling was a family activity. Mothers and sisters knew the sport, the moves, and the scoring, often better than the men of the family.

It did not take the couple long to learn how to host a potluck barbeque in Cresco. Delegated by the wrestling mothers, Lori provided tables and set out the condiments and buns. Tom pressed out the hamburger patties and fired up the Kingsford charcoal briquettes in a precise manner his team fathers requested. He readied the grill for them as they gladly took over the responsibilities for the burgers and hotdogs when they arrived. The wrestling mothers took care of the rest, including the Kool-Aid punch they named by color, not its flavor. Each mother appeared with her particular specialty and knew her responsibility for what to bring to the potluck. The feast always seemed to have potato salad with plenty of sliced-up hard-boiled eggs and Miracle Whip mayonnaise, and German potato salad made with bacon and vinegar. Baked beans with bits of bacon, plus a variety of fresh garden salads and chips filled the table. A Jell-O salad with fruit or marshmallows formed in a Bundt cake pan had a particular spot next to the brownies and lemon bars.

Even though Lori encouraged the families to take home the leftovers, her refrigerator ended up stacked full. Additional purchases of Tupperware containers allowed her the freedom from spending the following weeks returning dishes. She valued the opportunity to become more acquainted with the wrestling mothers, but carving out time became complex as her position as state social worker expanded. Often the demanding life of a farmer's wife left them socially isolated, especially during the hectic summer months. Lori believed a few mothers left their dishes intentionally to have a visitor come to their farm. She happily obliged them whenever possible, even if she didn't have a serving bowl or pan to return.

In the fall, small bands of grapplers appeared at their house in the evenings or on Sunday afternoons to hang out or watch football on television. Lori used the opportunities to engage the teens in continual conversations regarding weight control and cutting weight. Many of them disclosed to Lori how they fasted for two or three days, ran in rubber suits, and crawled under the wrestling mats to sweat out the last few pounds. The teenagers shared stories of how wrestlers used whirlpools, the local hotel's sauna, and how they stuck their fingers down their throats to force themselves to throw up any food they consumed. Lori tried to convince them of the need for long-term diets, counting calories and good nutrition, emphasizing staying

35

hydrated by drinking plenty of water. Someone always brought up the lore of the grappler who took a laxative to lose weight, which did not take effect until suddenly halfway through his match. A vast "Ugh!" rose, followed by belly laughter rocketing the room.

CHAPTER 4
DREW

If Iowa could be considered the center of wrestling in the United States, Waterloo, Iowa would be the center of Iowa wrestling, with over twenty state championship teams between the two large high schools. But in 1972, representing the hundreds of small farm towns in Iowa, Cresco, with a population under 3,000 people, with seven state team championships and over fifty individual state champions, would be at the top of the wrestling list.

Replacing Chris Flannigan, a Hall of Fame Coach, was almost impossible, but Tom felt up to the challenge with his experience at Cooper High School. Coach Flannigan never had a losing season in twenty-five years at the Spartan wrestling program's helm, but he left the cupboard nearly empty by Cresco's standards. The Spartans concluded their previous season with nine wins and two losses in dual meets, losing only to West Waterloo and Waverly. Coach Flannigan took five wrestlers to the state tournament, three of them received medals, and Cresco finished in the top ten as a team. The senior-dominated squad graduated four of those state qualifiers along with two other starters. Bing Natvig, a runner-up as a sophomore, returned as the only state qualifier for Coach Kilmer's rookie year. Drew Parker wrestled at 167-pounds as a sophomore, winning 18 matches and losing seven, and missed qualifying for the state tournament by one match.

With Bing and Drew as experienced juniors, Tom expected five unproven seniors in his varsity line-up as head coach of the Cresco Spartans. Three of the seniors chose not to turn out for their senior year. Even though they made the line-up, the other two were mediocre, not providing the leadership the coach hoped for from seniors and caused issues by 'dragging their feet' in response to new routines by the new coach. Other than Drew and Bing, the rest of the Spartans were young and inexperienced, and the squad got off to a poor beginning, losing their first five dual meets before winning four in a row.

The Cresco Spartans finished the dual meet season losing a remarkably close dual meet to conference champion Waverly 30 to 24. The first losing dual meet season for the Spartans in twenty-eight years, but the squad vastly improved over the season. Bing and Drew would be number one seeds going into the postseason. Coach Kilmer felt particularly encouraged with David "Hoss" Erickson, his heavyweight, and Charlie making it to the state tournament. It appeared reasonable with four or five Spartan wrestlers qualifying for the state meet, the team could finish in the top ten on the team board, then all would be well again in Cresco.

Joel and Karla Parker moved to Cresco as Drew entered third grade and encountered the difficulty of developing friendships in a small town where peoples' lives were already busy, intertwined with their extended family activities, community events, and church functions. Joel and Karla were the first parents to reach out to the new coach and his wife. They arrived at Tom and Lori's with pizza and a bottle of wine the day the Kilmers landed with their U-Haul trailer. Though the men did not share each other's passions, their friendship evolved from there. Joel didn't care for fishing, and Tom never golfed in his life, but they found they both rooted for the Minnesota Vikings and enjoyed playing cards squaring up to play Cribbage or recruiting their wives to join them in a game of '500'. In the fall, the Kilmers joined the Parkers attending Drew's football games which usually included dinner before the game and ended at one or the other's home. Karla and Lori became incredibly close during the wrestling season as they spent hours collectively at meets and tournaments.

Three days before the postseason began with the sectional tournament, Joel Parker died in a horrendous car accident. Joel served as the county hospital director in Cresco, and Karla worked as a nurse in nearby Decorah. Joel decided to surprise his spouse for lunch. Where the highway heads down an extended slope winding around the limestone bluffs just outside Decorah, he swerved to miss a farm tractor pulling out onto the road. Joel hit a patch of ice and slid head-on into an oncoming Kenworth semi-truck, dying on the impact.

The Decorah Hospital, where Karla Parker worked, sprang into crisis mode when the emergency responders notified the hospital of the name and the status of the person they were transporting. By chance, Lori Kilmer, on her job as a state social worker, entered the hospital to meet with a client as the news of Karla's husband raced through the hallways. She hurried to find her friend and traced Karla to the administrative office where the chief nurse consoled her. When Karla spotted Lori, she made a relatively calm request, through her red eyes and a scared voice, "Lori, Lori, call Tom. He has to get Drew out of school."

Lori's phone call triggered the high school principal to tear to the gym to notify Tom. In turn, the coach rushed to find Drew, pulled him out of class, and brought him to the office. Mystified by his coach's mission, Drew sensed something and silently walked with him to the counseling office. Alongside the school counselor, Tom informed Drew what happened to his father, and Drew collapsed in the coach's arms.

Joel Parker's death devastated his son and the entire team and took Tom to an emotional low, losing his friend. Tom found the courage to comfort his grapplers but felt no need or energy to motivate them for a tournament, no matter its significance. Drew scratched from the sectional tournament. Charlie, with two other starters, did not make weight and did not participate. Losing to two rivals he pinned during the dual meet season, Hoss's season ended. Bing waltzed through the tournament as the only Spartan wrestler to advance to the district tournament and then on to the state tournament.

Others looked to Drew in any sport as their leader, but he starred on the Spartan football team. He excelled as a football player for Cresco, not traditionally a football town, starting at running back and strong safety since his sophomore year. The Waterloo Courier newspaper named him an honorable mention all-state defensive back as a sophomore and first-team all-state defensive back following his junior season. In the spring, Drew ran track as a sophomore and placed fourth in the 100-yard dash, and finished third in the 200-yard race at the state tournament. Drew's pedigree contained athletic genes as his father played defensive end for Luther College. His mother, an outstanding sprinter, competed for a select track program in St. Paul during her teen years.

Standing six-foot-one inch, Drew weighed two hundred pounds. The speedy, sandy-blonde-haired stud loved the contact involved with football. College football coaches across the Midwest took notice. Drew's first love belonged to football. He wrestled because it is what you do in Cresco, Iowa, and success on the mat came extremely easy for the athlete. He built a special relationship with Tom and Lori Kilmer over the last year.

Subsequently to the accident, Drew and his mother spent many hours with the Kilmers. Karla much appreciated them for providing the needed support and relationship. Through her church, she retained a counselor and engrossed herself in a support group for dealing with her grief and worked through it, but Drew refused any counseling. Sometimes Drew showed up at Tom and Lori's home by himself to watch TV and not say a word. Other times, he babbled on about his father. Then there were times he needed to cry. He fell asleep on the couch more than a few times, and Lori would cover him with a blanket, call his mother, and let him spend the night. Drew skipped the spring track season, but he refocused on football again by the end of the school year.

Going into his second year at the Spartan wrestling program's helm, Tom Kilmer, aware of his coaching hot seat, seemed to have to defend his expectations for the upcoming wrestling season everywhere he stopped in town. As much as he desired to dodge the discussion, he could not avoid it. Whether it was ordering a pork tenderloin sandwich at the Stop Light Café, filling with gas at the Farm Service Station, or picking up freshly sliced chopped ham at the West End Grocery Store, someone always asked him a question revolving around the team. On Saturday mornings, Tom forced himself to go to the Main Street Diner for a cup of coffee with the collection of informal boosters who showed up there for years. The community understood how Joel Parker's death affected the wrestling team, but a short memory and high expectations erased the sympathy. The losing season left a bad taste in the mouths of the wrestling fans of Cresco. Drew Parker would be critical for the success of Tom's team and, maybe, for Tom maintaining his job.

CHAPTER 5

SPIDER

It seems every kid, especially in rural towns, acquires a nickname such as a shorter version of their first or last name, a physical trait, or as simple as adding 'y' to their name. Some nicknames last a short while, and some last a lifetime. The Spartan wrestling program, over the years, listed Buzzy, Bones, Sparky, Vandy, Lardo, Scooter, Toad, and many more on the roster. This Cresco squad was no different with Bingo, Whitey, Hoss, Rollie, Squirrel, and now Beaner. Referring to his size, Dave Erickson obtained his nickname in grade school when his buddies initiated calling him Hoss, referring to the large cowboy on their favorite TV western show, "Bonanza." Two athletes on the squad had never been tagged with a nickname. One of them was Drew Parker. Most people falsely assumed Drew was short for Andrew. The other one was Spider Westby.

Spider's father, Ken Westby, won a state

championship in 1938 as a freshman at 119-pounds. Wrestling fans of the time say he might be the toughest and meanest wrestler pound-for-pound Cresco ever produced. He only lost one match the entire year at the season's onset to a senior from Osage. When they wrestled again in the state finals, Ken destroyed him 16-5. The local newspaper, The Cresco Plain Dealer, reported Ken should have pinned him three different times, but it appeared he kept pulling the Osage Green Devil off his back just to beat up on him some more.

Ferociously, he relished physically punishing his opponents as he wrestled with such hatred for whoever dared challenge him. The anger carried over into school, resulting in numerous suspensions for fighting. The farm kept Ken's father too busy to attend even one of Ken's wrestling matches. He saw no need for school and resented Ken for turning out for the sport because it took him away from helping on the farm. After the wrestling season ended, followed by another suspension, his father professed enough was enough and pulled Ken out of school before the end of his freshman year, right before Ken turned sixteen. When Japan attacked Pearl Harbor less than three years later, Ken joined the army to beat up on the Japanese.

World War II did not go Ken's way, however. Being captured at the battle of Bataan, where nearly 78,000 United States and Filipino soldiers surrendered to the Japanese, Ken became a fraction of the Bataan Death March, forced to walk over sixty miles without food or water to the POW camp known as Camp O'Donnell. More than 500 U.S. soldiers and over 6000 Filipino soldiers died along the way due to brutal treatment by the Japanese Imperial Army.

Ken never spoke a word of the Death March nor the nearly three years he spent as a prisoner of war. When Ken came home, many locals thought the horror of incarceration sucked the anger out of him. Ken kept to himself, occupying his time with farm work and attending church on Sundays. Both his parents died within two years of Ken returning home. First, his father and then ten months later, his mother passed away. Ken began coming into town more often, spending time drinking with other veterans at the American Legion Hall bar.

Sadie's parents and Ken became acquainted during the coffee time following church, and they introduced him to their daughter. After graduating from high school, the expectations for Sadie were finding a husband, moving out of her childhood home, and starting a family. Ken appeared to be a perfect fit. He was a good Lutheran and likely needed someone to cook, care for him, manage the house, and help with the chores. Ken and the much younger Sadie married that summer, as a matter of convenience, not love. The newlyweds anticipated having a large family of boys to help with the family farm, and Ken looked forward to teaching them the sport of wrestling.

The rage returned as Ken spent more time with the bottle than working his farm. The demons from the war he refused ever to discuss and a wife who gave him three daughters instead of sons swelled the resentment inside him.

Sadie's family, neighbors, and friends held suspicions regarding Ken's treatment of her but found it too taboo to talk aloud. The physical work of chores on a farm resulted in an occasional bruise here and there but not the constant bruises or red marks on Sadie's face. But she always voiced an excuse for each one. Ken slowly quit attending church, but Sadie did not miss a Sunday service with the three girls in tattered dresses. Pastor Johansen of the Immanuel Lutheran Church kept an eye out for Sadie and her children and, along with other church members, slipped her some money now and then, or they would send a casserole or a dessert home with her. Embarrassed in acknowledging her need, Sadie gratefully accepted the charity on behalf of her children.

Pregnant with their fourth child, Sadie packed up the farmhouse when the mortgage company repossessed the farm and, with the help of her brothers, moved into an old rental house across from the dirt racetrack at the fairground. Ken worked as a farmhand and occasionally worked in town doing custodial work while spending his evenings at the Legion Hall drinking Seagram's

Seven. Convinced Sadie would have another daughter; Ken did not stay at the hospital. He checked her in for the delivery and left. He did not have many happy days in his life, but the day Sadie introduced him to his newborn son was special. Ken celebrated by passing out cigars all over town and bragging he had a son. When people asked the baby's name, he told them Sadie would be naming him.

The girls stayed with Sadie's parents during her hospital visit. Two days following the birth of his son, Ken picked up his daughters from his in-laws. He took them to Sydney's Gift and Flower Shop and picked out flowers for their mother before heading to the hospital to bring their new brother home. Ken and the girls were all smiles as they entered the hospital room. He bathed, shaved, and put on a button shirt. Clutching the mason jar of the fresh flowers, Ken and the giggling girls waited to find out what Sadie named their brother. Sadie held her son in her arms, delighted in seeing her family, and for a moment, she truly hoped that her family would be a real family now that they had a son. Before Sadie revealed his name, Ken noticed the birth certificate on the table next to the hospital bed.

"What the hell? You named him JAN? You gave MY boy a God damn girl's name!!!"

A name, the only thing Sadie controlled enough to pass on, representing her proud Norwegian heritage and a chance to honor her loving father. Sadie tried to tell Ken the name Jan, pronounced "Yonn," an abbreviated form of Johan, was her grandfather's name and her father's middle name. Ken threw the jar of flowers across the room. When it shattered against the wall, the girls raced to their mother, huddled around her, clutched her pleated skirt. They witnessed this scene too many times before and were petrified of what might happen next. Tears streamed down their faces. Sadie, who always tried to remain strong for her children, wept openly, too.

"Jan," the rant continued. "A God damn girlie name! What the hell are you thinkin'? He's goin' grow up and be a man... he'll need a real name. Look at HIM... he's got them big hands already, with long frickin' spider fingers and...."

Sober enough to remember telling everyone in town Sadie named their son, Ken abruptly snatched the birth certificate and the pen off the nightstand. He inked in the word Spider in front of the name Jan. Leaving the name Jan may have been the only respectful thing he ever did for his wife. With that act, Spider Jan Westby became official.

"His name is Spider. Got that, girls?" They nodded. "Nobody calls him J-A-N unless they wanna get knocked on their ass! Ya understand?"

They nodded again through their sobbing.

Spider Jan Westby grew up rapidly learning to hide any physical pain because it only created more. Still, Spider's personality held an

50

exceptionally soft, loving, and caring side he inherited from his mother. Learning the hard way, he kept this trait a secret from his father.

Pastor Johannsen was the only other person besides his mother and his grandparents to call him Jan. When a seven-year-old Spider heard a church elder refer to Pastor Johannsen as Pastor Jan, he snuck into the church office. Finding a letter addressed to the Reverend Jan Johannsen, he smiled.

Ken taught Spider how to wrestle, 'more like how to fight,' on the living room floor. Treating Spider no different than anyone else he wrestled, the lessons often ended in tears, with Sadie having to stop her husband somehow. Most of the house's second-hand furniture needed some repairs because Spider landed on or bounced off it. A small stack of outdated phone books supported the couch's back corner where the leg broke off. Sadie's brother cut a piece of plywood and placed it under the couch's cushions in the living room to prevent the broken springs from pushing through. On one side of the sofa stood a floor lamp with no lampshade. On the other side of the couch, a cracked porcelain lamp with a crooked shade sitting on a small end tabled dimly lit the room. One of her brothers made Sadie's prize possession, the oval white oak coffee table, crafted out of her grandparent's dining room table. It had seen far better days considering Spider had been dropped on the top of it like in a barroom cowboy fight, and it split down the middle. It needed to be repaired again for the fourth time.

A small black and white television with a vinyl case held collectively by duct tape rested on the top of bookshelves constructed of weathered barn boards and supported and separated by burnt clay bricks from the farm. The television received two channels, and sometimes a third channel if the rabbit ears antenna, wrapped in aluminum foil, were turned just right.

The only picture on the dingy leaf-patterned wallpapered walls in the living room was an eight-by-ten black and white photo of Sadie and the kids. Its reglued wooden frame held a cracked pane of glass over the front of the picture. Her parents purchased a copy of the picture from a photographer the church hired to compile the church directory. Sadie loved the photograph because all four of her children wore genuine smiles.

A decrepit reclining chair that did not recline sat in the corner next to the couch, opposite the television. Plastic sheets were tacked over the single-pane windows throughout the house to help shield out the winter weather. A plaid blanket acted as a door to their shared bedroom, giving the girls a touch of privacy from the living room.

Spider had a six-foot by ten-foot room, which was barely large enough for his bed. One wall had a small window, and there was no closet. A metal-framed rack on wheels for hanging the few clothes he owned, parked across from his bed against the wall. He kept his one extra pair of shoes, a second-hand pair of work boots, neatly under his bed next to a cardboard box containing his wrestling gear. Spider kept his underwear, socks, and a couple of t-shirts in an old wooden fruit crate under the other end of his bed.

Sadie kept the kitchen immaculately clean and organized as she loved cooking and baking. The only thing appearing out of place might be a row of five or six marshmallows, which sporadically showed up on the window ledge above the sink. Spider liked marshmallows when they turned crusty and chewy on the outside but remained soft and sweet on the inside. When Sadie had spare money to splurge on marshmallows, she surprised Spider and lined up a few of them on the ledge to dry out.

Most evenings, the kids gathered around the kitchen table and helped their mother with the cooking and cleaning chores at dinner time. The girls set the table. Spider helped clear the table when they completed their meal and took the garbage out while his mother washed the dishes and his sisters swept the floor and helped dry and put the dishes away. If their father happened to be home for dinner, Sadie took over all the kitchen cleaning duties and excused the children, who directly hid in their bedrooms to stay out of sight of their dad.

Spider treasured his time in the kitchen with

his mother especially making Lefse, a Norwegian flatbread made from mashed potatoes and cream. His mother gave him the title of 'Chief Roller' with the responsibility of rolling the potato dough out into a thin sheet resembling a foot-wide circle. His mother then fried it on a grill using a special stick her mother had given her for flipping the Lefse over on the grill. Spider loved to eat it warm and covered it with butter. When it melted, he sprinkled it with plain sugar and rolled it up. The kitchen's happy sounds were few and far between but even more seldom after his sisters moved out of the house.

When not learning wrestling by clashing with his dad, he sharpened his talent in the summer at the park next to the tennis courts and on the Methodist Church's lawn across the street from the American Legion Hall.

Ken had more than a few car accidents, so when Sadie felt Spider grew old enough, Sadie would send Spider to the Legion Hall to ensure Ken made it home safely. He walked the mile and a quarter downtown to wait outside the hall or in the car for his dad. In the summertime, Spider always seemed to find a few other boys his age clustered outside the hall also waiting for their fathers. Running their errands to such places as the farm supply store, the bank, or the grocery store, their fathers ended up stopping by the Legion Hall for a beer or two, visiting with friends before heading back to the farm.

Spider recognized most of the boys and usually addressed them by name. During the summer, someone, sooner or later, challenged another to a wrestling match, and the evening's competition under the tall oak trees began. These wrestling matches tended to be more like brawls and did not have the general "rules of conduct" which happened at the park. Matches did not end with a takedown and did not necessarily stop even when someone got pinned. The loser had to "cry uncle" to give up. Sometimes the contest turned to blows, but even then, the boys ended up shaking hands at the end of each battle.

Not necessarily fond of the combat ingredient of these matches, Spider did not back down from any of it. But for the most part, as the smallest kid, he concentrated on using technique and leverage to control challengers. Every once in a while, a new kid took part. Sizing Spider up, they challenged him, thinking they had a little 'fish' to take down and dominate quickly. But ultimately, they were surprised as Spider used his quickness and leverage for takedowns, and he learned to throw his leg in for control while on top. He rode them for what seemed like forever by using a cross-face, an armbar, or a far side half nelson to keep them down until they gave up. The bigger boys, especially the newbies, got frustrated. When Spider let them up, they smacked him or at least tried. It did not bother Spider because he had been a victim of a lot worse. One by one, the boys disappeared with their fathers and went home. At the end of the nights, Spider waited alone.

It sounded funny, but Spider welcomed it when Ken was too drunk to drive. One of his dad's buddies or the bartender would help walk him out or cart him out and throw him in the back seat. The bartender would predictably rub the top of Spider's head, commenting, "Take care of him, Spider,...and be careful."

Besides not having to wrestle with him when Ken was too drunk or passed out, Spider got to drive the old Chevy Bel Air four-door sedan. Getting to drive was 'cool' for an eleven or twelve-year-old kid. Spider would jump behind the steering wheel, and his legs barely reached the pedals, making it challenging to manage the brake and clutch. He would grab the keys from above the sun visor, and off they'd go. He liked taking a longer way home, hoping his friends might see him driving. Spider and his mother let Ken sleep it off in the back of the car during good weather. Otherwise, they somehow walked him to bed.

Once in a while, police officers would pass by as Spider drove home. Seeing Spider in the driver's seat, they acknowledged him with a slight wave and went on with their business or, at times, followed Spider to the Westby household. The first time it happened, the officer pulled in the driveway behind Spider and stepped out of the patrol car. Spider, scared of being arrested, stayed in the car and, as silly as it seemed, locked the car door. Coming forward, the officer tapped on the driver-side window. Spider slowly rolled it down.

"You alright, Spider?"

"Umm....uh-huh, sure," Spider sighed, surprised the policeman knew his name. He opened the car door and waited for the handcuffs.

"Here, let me help you get your dad in the house."

It wasn't the first time a police officer carried Ken into the house and not the last.

"Just make sure you stay off Main Street and the highway. Okay?"

"Will do. Thanks."

Organized wrestling in Cresco did not begin until junior high school. The school district had one elementary school in town, and three other elementary schools located in the small communities outside of Cresco called Lime Springs, Elma, and Ridgeway. Spider's classmates doubled in numbers in seventh grade as the schools combined for junior high. Many of these students were on the school bus for up to an hour each way, making it more challenging to be involved in after-school activities. Most of the farm boys did not participate in track and field in the spring or football in the fall when the fieldwork of planting or harvesting demanded their time. Therefore, they did not have a lot of experience with team sports. But when wintertime arrived, they excelled at the individual physical work of the sport of wrestling. Spider knew some of them from his Legion Hall experience. He already earned their respect, and now they were his friends and teammates.

As a far superior athlete but smaller and not as vicious as his father, most fans still considered Spider a formidable wrestler. His technique developed from all the years of protecting himself and being conscious of where his hips needed to be to avoid getting taken down or giving up a reversal. This made him a stellar grappler. He learned head position and how to avoid significant blows. He had developed his ability to ride and control a foe, making it difficult to escape from because he was all over an adversary, like a 'SPIDER.'

Spider only had twenty total matches in junior high school. He won six matches and lost four as a seventh-grader and improved to seven wins with only three losses as an eighth-grader. This record did not provide him "bragging rights," but Spider never wrestled anyone his size. His junior high coach felt his best kid should wrestle the other school's best wrestler even if they were fifteen to twenty pounds heavier than Spider.

By the time Spider completed junior high school, his sisters were gone. His oldest sister dropped out of high school, married, and moved to Waterloo, where her husband began his career in the John Deere Plant assembling the 4020 tractors.

His other two sisters moved out of the house during high school and lived with friends until they graduated. Following high school, one sister moved to Mason City and worked as a waitress at the local Maid-Rite Café. The other moved to Minneapolis, attended beauty school, married her high school sweetheart, and started a family. None of them ever came home to visit, but at least one of them called their mother each week to check on her and Spider. They knew how badly their father treated Spider, and they knew Spider took it to protect their mother.

Spider had a goal to graduate from high school, but going to college never entered his mind. He worked hard in school to be a "C" average student. He rarely completed his homework. Many of his teachers told him that he would have received an "A" in their classes if he only did his homework. They became frustrated with him. His pride prevented him from telling them his father took his homework and threw it in the garbage or out the door, scorning him about not needing school, urging him to drop out to get a job just like his old man did. Spider instead shrugged off his teachers and acted as though he did not care. Most of his teachers gave up on him, but a few guessed his circumstances and continued to encourage Spider.

Coach Tom Kilmer was one of those teachers and often took the time to discuss with Spider his future goals. Though Tom taught in the high school, he frequently touched base with the junior high wrestlers. He anchored his teaching and coaching philosophy in building strong personal relationships with his students and wrestlers, believing students and athletes learn more, perform better, and achieve higher results by boosting their confidence. Tom reduced or eliminated their fear of failure by giving them the knowledge of a caring support system. He believed the more adults in a student's life supplying this support, the more successful they will be.

Tom possessed a genuine knack for connecting with teenagers and for identifying individuals who lacked adult support. It did not take long for the coach to identify Spider as one of those students who needed special attention. The junior high and high school buildings were side by side and shared common areas such as the gymnasium and cafeteria. Tom spent time in the cafeteria during lunch and connected with his student-athletes and future wrestlers. He always brought extra food and "accidentally" left it on the table for kids he knew were not getting enough at home. Spider became a nearly daily recipient of an apple, orange, or, better yet, one of Lori Kilmer's special ham, cheese, and lettuce sandwiches, which somehow appeared on his table.

Spider truly admired Coach Kilmer. They discussed topics other than school and wrestling. Spider loved to hear how the coach's dad taught

Coach how to fish. Coach Kilmer brought and shared with Spider his first Muddler Fishing Fly his father gave him. Spider could not remember ever getting a present from his father, not even for Christmas or on his birthday. The coach shared stories about his high school friend, Gary Keillor, now a storyteller on a Minneapolis radio station going by the name of Garrison. The coach brought his transistor radio to Spider and his friends to listen to Garrison's stories. They giggled at the sound effects Keillor used to enhance his presentations.

Besides fishing trips and the Minneapolis area sites, Spider loved to listen to Coach Kilmer talk about his college experiences, how his teammates won a national wrestling title, and the places he traveled. Spider dreamt of visiting Chicago, Wrigley Field, and the elevated rail system upon hearing the coach describe his trips there. Spider's most extended trip was when he traveled sixty miles to Mason City with his grandparents to visit his sister. Without knowing, the coach's genuine compassion gradually developed Coach Kilmer into a father figure for Spider Westby.

Spider embarked on his high school wrestling career weighing one hundred eleven pounds as the squad's third lightest boy. Spider's friend, Wes Sorenson, hoped to gain some weight by the onset of the season, but he still was the smallest kid on the roster at ninety-one pounds. Spider and Wes had not yet wrestled for Tom, but

61

they figured out they both played a crucial role for the coach's starting line-up at the lightest weight classes of 98-pounds and 105-pounds. Because of Spider's relationship with Tom Kilmer, he could not wait to display his talent for him as a high school wrestler.

CHAPTER 6

BEANER

The previous spring, Jose Rodriquez moved with his parents to work on the Spiegler Dairy. Jose learned to fight in the labor camps, sometimes out of fun but most of the time having to protect his belongings and, at times, his family. He learned to wrestle in Oklahoma by chance.

Jose's father, Arturo, brought his family to California from Mexico before Jose's birth as part of the federal Bracero program. Farmers and farm hands escaping the plains during the dust bowl, and young men returning from World War II headed to the cities for higher-paying occupations. The 1950s found farmers short of labor to plant and harvest crops. California desperately needed field workers. Due to the post-war economy driving a vast expansion of their garden crops, farms required a labor force, especially a cheap labor force. To help provide workers, the U.S. government negotiated the Bracero agreement with Mexico. The deal

63

allowed laborers to legally enter the United States for a limited time frame to work and return to Mexico at the end of the harvest season.

The Bracero program to the poor Mexican laborer contained promises of permanent work, decent wages, appropriate living conditions for families, and transportation back to Mexico. Not fooled by the propaganda, Arturo Rodriquez periodically found the conditions for his family despicable. Despite the conditions, life for his family and its future, though difficult, would be far better in the United States than life would ever be in returning to Mexico. Arturo had an advantage over most immigrants, having learned English from the parish priest in his village. This benefit of speaking English created more opportunities than he imagined would be possible.

During the twenty years of the Bracero agreement, over four million Mexican laborers entered the United States. Arturo, his wife Rosie, and their two young boys walked one hundred thirty miles to the border to sign up for the program. Through the Bracero program, the Rodriquez family legally entered California in the early spring of 1952. At the end of the growing season, his work contract expired, but he had no intent to return to Mexico.

Tens of thousands of illegal Mexican immigrants were coming over the border to work. Thousands of legal immigrants such as the Rodriquez family overstayed their work visas and were now in the United States illegally. In 1954, the government cracked down on illegal immigrants under an operative titled Operation Wetback. U.S. agents swept the fields and detained undocumented workers for deportation. Hundreds of daily raids resulted in busing thousands of illegals back to Mexico.

The long days of work, low wages, and the labor camp conditions were appalling. Many Bracero workers barely made enough money to pay the monthly rent in the labor camps for a dirt floor cabin and community restrooms, with many lacking showering facilities. Arturo used his ability to speak English to be an interpreter for farm foremen and negotiated free rent. By the end of his second season, working strawberries, asparagus, lettuce, and avocados in California, he saved enough money to buy a well-used 1948 Ford pickup truck. Arturo and Rosie built a homemade wooden camper shell over the pickup bed for the family to stay.

Arturo soon figured out working for a smaller farm operator kept him under the federal agents' radar. He stumbled upon an independent dairy farmer near San Jose needing winter help. A friend of the dairy farmer purchased an apple orchard business near Watsonville the following spring. For the next four years, Arturo moved his family back and forth seasonally between Watsonville and San Jose.

Both Arturo's older sons were born in their

village in Mexico in a shed they called home. In April of 1955, Arturo took his wife, Rosie, to a San Jose clinic, where she gave birth to their third son. With the help of a Hispanic physician and the clinic staff, Rosie and Arturo secured a birth certificate that verified U.S. citizenship for Jose Manuel Rodriquez.

In the early spring of 1960, when Arturo appeared at the orchard to work, the orchard owner met him at his truck with an envelope and commented, "Hey, Arturo, the Feds stopped by last week looking for illegals. I don't think they were looking for you...just trying to scare me. But you and I know they will be back. And you know what that means."

Arturo nodded understandingly. His experience told him his family would be detained and deported, and his boss would receive a hefty fine. The farmer continued, "Here's an address and letter to a friend running an apple orchard in Washington. He needs some hard workers if you're interested. I know it's a ways away, but here's a little bonus cash for your hard work. Gracias, good luck." They shook hands. The small bonus bought less than three tanks of gas as they headed north.

With Arturo's decision, the family moved to Wenatchee, Washington, where, with proof of U.S. citizenship, Jose enrolled school for the first time. The older brothers were tall enough to help with the orchard work. No one got paid by the hour. They contracted work by the job or the bushel of fruit, so the more hands picking or pruning, the more income the family received. Commonly staying no more than a couple of years in any one place, the Rodriguez family moved from Wenatchee to Walla Walla, Washington, to Twin Falls, Idaho, and then near Fort Collins, Colorado. Their experience with dairies provided yearlong work and avoided the more conspicuous fieldwork.

Along the way, Jose went to school, even if it was for a fragment of the year. Though he spoke English, Jose chose to say little of it to anyone at school because his family depended on him not to stand out. It was easy to do because most teachers and school principals assumed he had a limited understanding of the English language. Besides speaking English, Jose was adequately able to read and write English, but any display of advanced language intellect might make Jose conspicuous. Often schools initially enrolled him in remedial classes, but when teachers discovered his high ability, they often used him to tutor other Spanish-speaking students. Jose used his instructional competence at home to teach his family lessons he learned in school.

An essential layer of the Hispanic migrant community included its ability to communicate vital information by word-of-mouth, precise details regarding farmers looking for laborers to hire, farms with favorable working conditions, farms not to work on, federal agencies' activities, and supportive community resources. When living in Colorado, Arturo learned through this grapevine about a farmer from Iowa who had bought a dairy farm near Hobart, Oklahoma, and needed some hired hands. By the time Arturo, Rosie, and Jose arrived in Hobart, the older Rodriguez sons had gone on their own. The father and his son were immediately hired on the milking crew, and it did not take long for Rosie to be working right alongside her men.

Arturo purchased a different and newer pickup. By the fall, having a resident address on the farm, he felt comfortable going to the courthouse and registering his truck in Oklahoma. Taking such precautions relieved Arturo's fear of being pulled over for an 'out of state' or 'out of date' license plate.

Jose's eighth-grade physical education class in Hobart had a wrestling unit, and Jose received his first formal introduction to the sport. A quick study, he surprised himself how rapidly he learned the sport and began to beat students in the class with wrestling experiences. Watching Jose's success, the teacher recognized some natural abilities and balance and referred him to the high school wrestling coach.

Jose returned home to the shack at the dairy one day after school and talked to his father in Spanish, "Papá, the wrestling coach wants me to go out for wrestling. He took me to the high school today. He wanted me to see all the wrestling trophies in the trophy case. He showed me a picture of a boy who won the state last year. He is brown like you and me, Papá, but not a Mexican. He is an Indian. His name is Spottedbird. He is a champion, and the coach thinks I could be a champion!"

Arturo surveyed his son's twinkle of happiness in his eyes, spoke, "But Jose, we need you to help on the farm. We need you to earn money. How will we get the milking done without you here? Besides, if you are as good as the coach thinks you are, someone will not like it. They will make a phone call."

Jose was extremely protective of his parents and conscious of not bringing attention to his family. He knew even an anonymous phone call to the Immigration and Naturalization Services would eventually bring a visit from federal agents to the farm. Even with a birth certificate proving his United States citizenship, Jose never felt safe from detainment by INS agents. He heard many stories of Hispanics with legal documentations being swept up in raids and deported to Mexico.

"Please, Papá, I want to wrestle. I promise to work twice as hard when I get home. I will get up earlier and do more." Arturo, not budging, shook his head no. "Will you just let me practice with the team? I will not wrestle against other schools or do contests. I'll come home and do my job."

Arturo thought it through for a few days as Jose continued to plead his case and finally consented. "No competition, just practice. You must be home every night in time to help with clean up."

Jose did not realize the incredible opportunity he had to practice and learn wrestling at Hobart High School. He never missed a practice for two years. His daily practice included the opportunity to work out with three individual state champions.

Something spurred Arturo and his keen sense of the need to move on, and he let the dairy owner know his intention to leave Hobart. When his boss mentioned having a cousin in Iowa who needed an experienced milking hand, Arturo packed up the family. He headed northeast to the Spiegler Dairy outside the town of Cresco, Iowa, farther away from the Mexican border.

The timing was perfect as the hired hand left the farm to take a job at the manufacturing plant in town, leaving the cabin available for the Rodriguez family. The living conditions on Charlie Spiegler's parent's dairy farm far exceeded any shack they ever stayed in. The quarters sat between the barn and the primary home. The small front room extended into a kitchen area with a refrigerator and a wood-burning stove for heat and cooking. With indoor plumbing, the small bathroom even offered a tiny showering stall. A large storage area provided Jose with his own bedroom. Charlie's mother gave Rosie some old curtains to hang, and Rosie took great pride in keeping the cabin clean. As usual, the

Rodriquez crew went right to work with the efficiency of a well-oiled machine. The entire Spiegler family was incredibly impressed by the hard-working Rodriquez household.

Leaving the Hobart wrestling room disappointed Jose. He could compete with anybody in the room, beating most of them. Little did he know, the Spiegler Dairy in Cresco, Iowa, opened a more significant opportunity for him. The Spiegler family name had become synonymous with Cresco wrestling. At least one Spiegler boy, if not more than one, cracked the Spartan line-up every year for the previous fifteen years. The family and its extended clan produced three state champions and five state place winners as a feature of Cresco's rich wrestling history. The next generation of quality wrestlers defending the name of Spiegler included Charlie.

When Jose overheard Charlie discussing wrestling with his father, Greg, Jose's ears perked up. It took a week or so before Jose felt confident in mentioning to Charlie he had wrestling experience. Charlie did not think much of it but happened to bring up his conversation with Jose to his father one early summer evening at the supper table, "Did you know Jose is a wrestler? At least he said he was."

"Well, they came here from Oklahoma. Maybe he got a taste of it there. Why don't you drag him along with you on Friday nights and see what the hell he's made of? It might be an incentive for them to stay around next year. They are damn good workers, and I'd hate to lose them. You never know when they might get spooked and take off. Who knows, maybe he'd help the team out."

A week and a half before school began in Cresco, Coach Kilmer rolled up to the barn on Spiegler Dairy in time for the second shift of milking. With his work clothes on, the youthful coach entered the milking parlor.

"Hola, Coach! Charlie's not here."

"I'm not here to see Charlie. Thought you could use some help tonight."

Jose appeared puzzled and glanced at his father. "This is the wrestling coach I told you about. He wants to help us with the milking."

Arturo exchanged words with his son in Spanish, and Jose turned to Coach, "My papá says you should stay out of the way, or you'll get cow shit on those nice boots you have on."

Tom chuckled in response, "Probably a good idea! I'll help where I can. Hey, just let me know. Can I talk to you and your folks?"

"Okay, I understand and speak English some," interrupted Arturo, though apprehensive about letting on how well he spoke English. Rosie uttered something to Arturo in Spanish, and he continued, "We keep working, Coach. Okay? Dialogo...understand?"

"Si," was one of two words Tom knew in Spanish as he smiled at Rosie, who did not smile back, instead returned a skeptical stare. Tom spent over an hour with the Rodriguez family in the barn, talking fishing, farming, school, and wrestling. Amazed by how hard and efficient they worked, Tom found himself in the way more often than being helpful.

With the milking completed, Rosie whispered to Arturo, handed Tom the water hose with a spray nozzle, and walked out of the parlor. More than happy to lend a hand, Tom kept his boots clean as he sprayed down the stalls and walkway. Not until they completed washing the milking parlor did he discover why Rosie left early. Arturo insisted Tom join them on the small, covered porch on the front of the cabin. The three men sat on the edge of the porch with their feet on the ground. A beaming Rosie brought out plates and a pot full of tamales. Using a hot cloth mitt, she served two tamales to each of them. Tom never had tamales, and Jose observed his reluctance.

"Hey, Coach, the good stuff's on the inside," Jose shared. He demonstrated for Tom by partially unrolling the corn husk exterior and commenced eating the corn dough, called masa, Rosie cooked with chicken, onion, garlic, and chili powder. When Jose finished eating the guts of the tamale, he threw the corn husk on the gravel in front of the porch. Tom followed his lead and even took up Arturo's hot sauce offer, though he used it sparingly. Tom gradually realized he liked Mexican food or at least Rosie's tamales, and the Rodriguez family grinned at him as he accepted her offer of another one.

The conversation remained light, mostly talking about the farm. Though the trio shared information cautiously, it became apparent the Rodriguez family appreciated Coach Kilmer's visit, and they agreed to his proposal of helping them register Jose in school. Tom intentionally avoided questioning where they have lived, but Jose uncharacteristically spilled his guts regarding his wrestling experience in Oklahoma. It now made sense to the coach how Jose developed his advanced wrestling skills. In the back of his mind, Tom wondered if Jose would actually enroll in high school and still be in Cresco during the wrestling season. Rosie disappeared into the cabin and returned a few minutes later with some tamales wrapped in aluminum foil, insisting Tom take them home for Lori.

"Gracias," he used the other Spanish word in his vocabulary. The men exchanged handshakes, and Rosie surprised the coach by hugging him goodbye.

CHAPTER 7

BING

Leaving his wife sound asleep, Tom climbed quietly out of the other side of the bed at five o'clock, trying not to disturb her. All summer, he had a standing Monday morning fishing date with Bingo. He threw on his Levi's, a t-shirt, a light blue cotton long sleeve shirt he left unbuttoned, and silently headed towards the bedroom door. Lori rolled over. With her eyes still closed and with a small smile, she whispered, "How about a kiss?" Tom grinned, returned to the bed, and obliged her. "Have fun. Tell Lynette hello for me," as she rolled back over for another hour and a half of sleep.

As Tom walked through the kitchen, he grabbed his empty Thermos bottle off the top of the counter. He stopped on the back porch to snatch his fishing vest, hat, creel, and pole. Locking the door behind him, he hesitated and smiled to himself, knowing how people in Cresco rarely lock their doors. Thinking to himself, "When you live in the city, you develop different habits."

He sat down on the porch steps and slipped on his boots. He tied up his laces and headed to the back of the detached garage, where he manually raised the garage door. He opened the trunk to his green fastback Chevy Nova and strategically loaded his fishing gear. He backed out of the garage, stopped, got out of the car, and closed the garage door behind him. With the Thermos beside him, Tom headed north out of town. As the sunlight broke through the trees, Tom circled the Natvig home arriving at the back of the house. Noticing the lights still on in the barn, he put the Nova into park. Bing's fishing pole leaned against the side of the screened-in porch, and a coffee can sat on the ground next to the pole.

Joyful greetings rang out from the four younger Natvig fledglings as they bounced out the screen door in their rubber barn boots on their way to do their chores.

"Morning, Mr. Kilmer!"

"Hi, Coach."

"Good luck fishing today."

"Mom's got breakfast waiting for ya."

"Dad and Bingo should almost be done."

"Good morning to you guys!" he hollered back as he climbed out of his Nova. Over the scent of freshly cut hay and the odor of the barnyard, the whiff of bacon rolled past his nose as he reached back in the open car window to grab his Thermos off the bench seat. Lynette met him on the porch and embraced him. "Good morning. So glad to see you. It's going to be a beautiful day. Coffee's on."

"Hi, Lynette. Lori sends her love."

"Tell her hi for me and tell her she needs to stop by. It's been a while. The boys will be here any second. Fill your Thermos, and I'll start another pot," responded Lynette in a bossy, motherly tone as she led the coach into the kitchen.

They made chitchat regarding the weather as Tom began his routine filling his Thermos bottle, and Lynette set the table. He poured a separate cup before sitting down at his designated spot. Bill and Bing strolled in the door, and they shared greetings with the coach.

"Hope our luck is better today than last week!"

"I hope you found us better worms!" They laughed.

Tom's relationship with the Natvig family developed around the white and red checkered, plastic-coated tablecloth. Tom valued his time with the Natvigs, joining them for breakfast before heading out fishing with Bingo. Lynette initiated the weekly breakfast invitation cementing their friendship. Tom learned all about the Natvig family over bacon, sunny-side-up eggs, fried potatoes, and lots of coffee. The pictures and postcards covering the refrigerator door displayed the Natvig celebrations, travels, friends, and family, more than occasionally sparked Tom's interests.

The family took extreme pride as the third generation of Natvigs to own the farm. Bing planned on becoming the fourth-generation Natvig farmer to work this land initially homesteaded by his great grandfather Ingval and his wife when they immigrated from Norway in the late 1800s. Neighbors considered Ingval an exceptional farmer with an intense interest in maintaining the fertile soil. He annually rotated crops of corn with oats or hay and, in later years, with soybeans. Ingval used a set of draft horses and up-to-date field equipment, including a John Deere metal blade plow and a McCormick reaper, to complete the farm's fieldwork. The Natvig farm's early success allowed them to expand their acreage, and shortly after the turn of the century, become one of the first farms in the area to use a gasoline-powered tractor.

Bing's grandfather and father continued with the progressive ideology, continually upgrading machinery and bringing electric power to the farm by a generator eight years before the Rural Electric Cooperative provided the farm with electricity. Although grains provided the primary source of income for the Natvig farm, they kept the farm diverse, raising various types of livestock. The founding Natvigs had milking cows for personal milk consumption. Bing's grandfather chose to stay out of the commercial milk business because of the high investment and labor intensity which took significant time away from supporting the rest of the farm.

After finishing breakfast, Bing loaded his fishing gear and the coffee can of worms into Coach's car. The pair slowly headed down the uneven tractor path, bordering the cornfield fence line, to the pasture on the farm's far north edge. Coach Kilmer and Bing formed a special bond through their whispers as they stood on the low grassy banks atop the narrow meandering trout stream. Over the stillness of the morning, the fishermen heard the intermittent buzz of the dog-day cicada and the songs of robins, sparrows, and finches. Tom learned Bing's birth certificate read William Ingval Natvig III, named after his father and grandfather. While his grandpa preferred to be called Will and his father answered to Bill, Lynette decided to call him by his middle name, Ingval, which became Ing, and then Ing morphed quickly into Bing. Anyone who knew him in Cresco called him Bing or Bingo, and most did not know his formal name.

As a handsome adolescent with short brown hair and hazel eyes, he toned the muscles in his body from the daily hard work on the farm. At five foot nine and a hundred forty pounds, he could pick up a bale of hay weighing forty to fifty pounds and raise it over his head and throw it out the upper haymow door. He could carry a bale in each hand, walking them down the feeder aisle in the barn.

Flaunting his exceptional grip, Bingo crushed small apples in his oversized hands. To sustain his conditioning, he jogged the three miles to and from school every day instead of riding the school bus or driving.

Next to wrestling, Bing thrived in his agricultural classes at Cresco High School and often skipped his academic classes to keep repairing the farm machinery in the Ag Shop. Bing appreciated his time to display his mechanical and sheet metal skills and distinguished himself as the best welder in the school. Bing focused on improving his arc-welding technique but was intrigued by the business classes of managing a farm. He gained a greater understanding and respect for his father, grandfather, and even his great grandfather and their decisions for administering and expanding their farming enterprise.

Cresco High School had the largest chapter in the state of the Future Farmers of America, commonly known as the FFA. The organization supported the school and the community's agricultural experiences by providing Career Development Events for its student members. Through the continual encouragement of his advisor, the introverted Bing eventually ran successfully for the office of treasurer for the Cresco Chapter, became more involved with state and national competitions, and received the FFA 'American Farmer' degree in production. He wore his blue corduroy FFA jacket with a large circular logo on the back. His name was embroidered in yellow thread on his left chest, which he displayed with pride.

Bing never shared with anyone about the turning point of his wrestling career until he learned to trust Coach Kilmer. One particular fishing morning, he and his coach stood silently waiting for a tug on their line. Bing opened up, "Ya know, coach, I was pretty good in junior high school, lost only one match. But it was just about hanging out with my buddies after school. I didn't think about how good I could be. I remember the day Coach had the high school wrestlers come to work with us."

Aware of its value, Coach Kilmer continued the tradition by encouraging his high school guys to help the junior high wrestlers. Bing shared, "Robby Herd had just won his state championship and paired up with me. He tore me apart, not letting me do anything. He kept taking me down, pinning me, and then letting me back up just to do it again. I got so mad, I finally stayed down on the mat on my back, after getting pinned for the sixth time, staring at the ceiling with tears in my eyes."

"Ya know, Coach, he just stared at me and said, what the 'f' ya doing? I seen you wrestle. You got more skills than I ever f-in' had in junior high, but you're a frickin' weenie. If you wanna be a state champ, you have'ta learn not to give in to nobody. Not even for an f-in' second in a match or even at practice. You might get beat, but you never give it up. They have'ta take it from you. Don't be half-assed. Ya understand? Nobody can teach you mental toughness. If you don't wanna be a state champion, what the 'f' you here for?"

"I slowly climbed back up to my feet, curled back into my neutral stance, and got ready to go. Heck, he kept taking me down, but I made it harder and harder, fighting him off. He didn't pin me again, and I even got away from him once. I learned the lesson, and my life changed. I decided right then and there to be a state champion."

Bing qualified for the state tournament his freshman year and lost the title his sophomore year 3-2, giving up a last-second escape. In his junior year, Bing shockingly lost his balance and got caught in a head and arm throw in the first period. He fought off his back for over a minute to end the period but fell behind 5-0. He stormed back but lost the championship 8-7.

The fishing trips with Coach came to an end as the harvest season took over and school commenced. October seemed to arrive abruptly. It was not as strenuous as the summer work, but October remained a hectic month on the farm as the harvest concluded and everyone prepared for winter's harshness. Over the summer, the Natvigs raised two decent hay cuttings and part of a third, filling their haymow to the brim. The haymow in the upper level of the oversized red barn had been stacked strategically to the roof with over-lapping rectangular hay bales. The bumper hay crop enabled them to sell the excess to other farmers for additional income. The oats were harvested in August, while combining the soybeans took two weeks at the end of September. The corn harvest began in October. The Natvigs stored some oats and corn for livestock feed while selling the soybeans to the local grain elevator.

At the beginning of October, as a delegate, Bing attended the National FFA Convention in Kansas City, Missouri, and returned home in time to help combine the corn. The corn used to be harvested by the ear and stored in the large wooden lath corncrib. The Natvig's newer combine shelled the corn off the ear, making it ready for the market or bin storage. Tearing the wood corncrib down went onto the 'to do' list as a winter project if the weather and time allowed. The destruction project has remained on the list for three years, as Bing reminded his dad. His father responded with a smirk, "Well, if you don't make it to state, YOU'LL have plenty of time to get that crib torn down while I'm in Des Moines watching your buddies!"

Bill Natvig had expanded the Angus beef herd to twenty cattle, nearly double what they raised five years earlier. They could not feed any more than twenty cattle and their other livestock due to the limited amount of hay and corn they stored for the winter. Calves born in the spring were weaned from their mothers during September and ready for the sale barn. Bill intentionally selected a quarter of the heifers to supplant older cows sold or sent to the butcher for slaughter to feed the family. In the fall, the herd was brought from the farm's pastures to the cement feedlot next to the barn, where they were fed twice daily. The Natvigs moved the herd inside the barn when the full brunt of winter arrived.

The combine, baler, and grain wagons needed to be serviced, cleaned, and undercover for the winter. They regularly serviced the tractors, using them throughout the winter moving snow and keeping the barn lot clean. The younger children prepped the chicken coop by cleaning out the coop and refreshing it with new hay. The chickens provided the family with fresh eggs for the breakfast table and a few extra dozens to sell a week. The Natvig kids were active in the local 4-H Club and raised a pair of pigs named "Wilma and Wilbur," who were paraded for judging at the Howard County Fair during the summer. Though the kids raised the hogs like pets, they understood Wilma and Wilbur, like the rest of the farm's pigs, provided lard, ham, chops, pork roasts, sausage, and bacon for the kitchen table. Farm children understood the cycle of life and its importance for the survival of the family. The horn of plenty from the garden and four apple trees put an abundance of carrots, tomatoes, peas, beans, rhubarb, apples, and potatoes in storage in the root cellar or were canned.

The workload decreased somewhat during the winter. Bing helped his dad, Bill, feed the hogs and cattle before school. His sisters fed the chickens and collected the eggs while the younger brothers made sure the corn and feed bins were kept full. Bing's mother, Lynette, found a part-time job in town during the winter to bring in needed cash to support the family. She saved her sewing jobs for the winter, patching jeans, darning socks, and making dresses for the girls.

But something was different this October. Usually, the first person up at five in the morning and out to the barn to feed the livestock, Bing found it more challenging to climb out of bed each morning. His mother, already in the kitchen working on breakfast, cackled about beating him to the kitchen. It bothered him. He knew his routine down to the minute, and he noticed things were taking more time. Even the run to school took nearly a minute longer than in August. Bing decided he must not be working hard enough, and to be a state champion, he needed to pick up his pace. But no matter how hard he concentrated and pushed his body, he saw no difference.

CHAPTER 8

PRACTICE

The Spartan wrestling room was more extensive than most high school wrestling rooms. It supported two 28 by 28-foot wrestling mats on the floor laid wall-to-wall with six-foot-tall grey pads hanging on the cinder block walls around the room. The wall pads, old gym mats made of canvas with smashed horsehair inside, hung by hooks, offered some protection from the hard concrete but easily fell off their hooks if a wrestler landed hard against them. The fifteen-foot high ceiling had exposed horizontal metal trusses. A row of one-foot tall windows ran along the ceiling's edge on one side wall letting in some natural light during the day. A gas heater with a blower hung from a truss in the far corner of the room, and during practices, the coaches set its thermostat at eighty degrees.

Built into the room were two stations for improving arm strength. Next to the entrance, a two-foot-wide pegboard hung vertically on the wall and extended from six feet off the floor to nearly the twelve-foot mark. Two rows of an inch in diameter holes ran parallel up the board. A wrestler clutched in each hand a solid metal six-inch-long peg with a red bicycle grip handle to climb up by moving one peg and then the other up the rows of holes in the board. Spider was a natural, controlling his body weight with one arm while swinging himself like a monkey to the other side. Back and forth, he scooted up and down the board, inserting the pegs. The heavier the body, the more challenging it seemed to be for a wrestler. Bingo worked his way up and down while Drew intermittently made it up the board. Hoss cursed when anyone mentioned the pegboard.

A braided manila climbing rope, approximately an inch and a half in diameter, hung from the ceiling in the front corner. The cord hooked high on the wall, out of the way when not in use. Though not a drill often initiated during the season, the wrestlers climbed by using their arm strength and a leg wrap technique. Most of the guys mastered the method to climb the rope to the top, but Bingo used the rope to show off as he climbed the rope using only his arms with his legs pointing forward, bent at his hips, and perpendicular to his body. Hoss, of course, cursed when anyone mentioned rope climbing.

The wrestling mats on the floor were navy blue with the bottom side up. Painted on that side of each mat were four, ten-foot in diameter, white wrestling circles. Inside each circle were two white lines designating the starting point for the down position, and at the end of the lines were two perpendicular strips of tape, one green and the other red. These foot-long lines were three feet apart, and competitors needed to have a shoe on a line when wrestling began in the neutral starting position.

During practices, the cold, cream-colored walls developed a thick layer of condensation from the high humidity created by sweaty bodies. Chips of paint easily peeled off the walls in many places. At the far end of the wrestling room, painted in sizeable black letters on the wall above the mats, read the title, "Cresco Wrestling." Under the title, a line stated, "Home Of." Stacked further underneath on separate lines were the phrases: "3 Olympic Wrestlers," "9 NCAA National Champions," "7 Iowa State Team Championships," "55 Individual State Champions," and "1 Nobel Peace Prize Winner."

Listed on the sidewall opposite the windows were fifty-five state champions' names with the year and the weight of the accomplishment. A person entered the high school wrestling room in Cresco, similar to entering a church's doors, with silent respect and acknowledgment of the people honored on the wall.

Some names were up on the list twice, and a few names appeared three times. Any Spartan can tell you about them with little difficulty, especially Don Maland, Gary Kurdelmeier, Tom Peckham, or Don Nichols. The last name listed belonged to Lee Johnson 1969 119#, a two-time state champion. The only name on the wall not having a state championship title behind it was Norman Borlaug. Borlaug wrestled for the Spartans and followed his high school coach to the University of Minnesota, wrestling for the Gophers in the 1930s. Achieving a Bachelor of Science degree and a Doctorate, he thrived in his work with the Rockefeller Foundation. He developed high-yielding and disease-resistant varieties of wheat, helping feed millions of people around the world. For his accomplishments, Borlaug received the 1970 Nobel Peace Prize.

Each boy entering the wrestling room dreamt of being the next name on the list, and many alumni sadly reminisced the mistakes preventing their names from being a piece of this elite fraternity. It is a significant achievement to place in the Iowa High School State Wrestling Tournament. The list would be four times in length if it included all the Spartan wrestlers who received a medallion while standing on the tournament podium. Bing Natvig being one of them, having lost twice in the finals, finishing second the last two years. This year would be different. He hated the list, and not seeing his name up there made him even more than determined to win a title.

As a motivational tool, Coach Kilmer

periodically used one of the prestigious grappler's stories of the adversities they overcame to achieve their accomplishment. Following the coach's inspirational story of Norman Borlaug's persistence and determination, Charlie responded thoughtfully, "Jeez, I gotta be a state champ to get up there, cause there ain't no way in hell I'll ever win a Nobel Peace Prize." The squad exploded in laughter, and Coach Kilmer almost choked on his gum.

The first day of wrestling practice at Cresco High School brought new excitement and anticipation to the program. The overall wrestling season can feel extensive and grueling, and the practices, hard and physical. Most wrestlers suffered a few bumps, bruises, bloody noses, or swollen lips and occasionally witnessed dislocations, knee injuries, concussions, severe sprains, or even broken bones during the season. Few activities during practices would be called fun. The few games they played, such as mat football on their knees or a form of tag the wrestlers called 'Slap Back,' usually ended up with someone hurt or pissed off, and then a coach stepped in before it turned into a brawl.

Despite the brutal competition throughout the season, the camaraderie of the wrestling team brought kids out. Twenty-eight "wanna-be" state champions made their way into the wrestling room as Tom's assistant coach, Joe Hall, opened boxes of headgear and knee-pads to check out to each individual. The wrestlers formed parallel lines and

91

waited for their turns.

Bing Natvig did not play football, so he showed up for practice the first day. The senior walked into the room, strolled up to the box, and grabbed the headgear with his initials on it. He investigated the knee-pad box and did not see what he wanted to see. He scanned the room and noticed an underclassman sitting against the wall with headgear and knee-pads. Bing hollered at him. "Hey, Squirrel, the black knee-pad is mine!"

The sophomore hopped up and dashed over to Bing and gave him the black knee-pad. "Sorry," and he sheepishly grabbed an old, ragged knee-pad out of the box. Feeling downhearted, he returned to his spot on the sidewall.

The two other returning lettermen who had followed Bing upfront collected their gear. Spider Westby positioned himself in line with the other freshmen, content to wait his turn while eying his father's name up on the wall. The freshmen were all apprehensive and intimidated by the upperclassmen. A brown Hispanic boy hung out by the entry door all alone, dressed in his worn but clean physical education shirt and gym shorts Coach Kilmer salvaged for him out of the lost and found bin. Jose would wait patiently.

The good Christian people of Cresco would shudder to think their actions could be construed as bias. With no one to identify it for them, they did not recognize the subtle racism of the Mexican jokes they told each other or the exclusion and avoidance of the Rodriquez family during the little time the Mexican family spent around town. Even when Arturo, Rosie and Jose attended weekly mass at the catholic church, no one sat beside them, and few people spoke to them.

Jose was the only student of Mexican descent in the high school. During lunch at school, Jose usually sat by himself. Once in a while, Charlie or a couple of wrestlers from the summer gatherings joined him, but they felt uncomfortable engaging Jose in conversation. Teachers had limited academic expectations for Jose and never called on him to answer a question. Though most teachers addressed him as Jose, many of them did not think twice when students referred to him as Beaner. One teacher, thinking he was one of the guys, openly called him Beaner during class.

Jose appreciated speaking Spanish in his interactions with the Spanish language teacher, Mrs. Gassett. They shared a laugh as they realized no one in Cresco would ever believe that the teacher was the only one between the two of them who had ever been to Mexico. Before she married and moved to Cresco, Mrs. Gassett spent three summers living in Saltillo, Coahuila, teaching English to Mexican students.

Eighteen-year-old Jose would shortly be on his own and would be making his own choices in life. His father knew this and asked Charlie to keep an eye out. With Iowa so far from the Mexican border, it may be possible that Arturo would end up back in Mexico and would not have a way to watch over or help Jose. Charlie's oversight would help ease Arturo's mind.

Unsure of how others would respond, Jose leaned against the wall by the wrestling room entrance, not wanting to make a scene. Jose would wait until last and take what was left after everyone else checked out their gear, going through the usual procedure. He contained his excitement of having his father's permission to challenge for a starting position on the varsity line-up and compete against other schools.

Bingo sat at the back of the room, chatting with his buddies, and suddenly noticed Jose standing by himself. Bing stood up and sauntered over to the headgear box. A freshman stood over the box with a substantial grin as he picked up the last set of brand new four-strap headgear, still in its clear plastic shipping bag. Bing took the bag from the kid's hands without saying a word and threw it to Jose. Proceeding back to his friends, Bing continued his conversation as though nothing had happened. Though most of the other wrestlers were aware of Jose from Friday nights in the park, Bingo's subtle act of leadership created a proclamation to everyone in the room to respect not only Jose's skills but Jose as a person. Jose would not be last again, at least not in the wrestling room. The poor freshman, who just lost a prize possession, panicked and hastily explored the box for a decent set of worn-out headgear in the slim pickings which remained.

Earlier, Coach Kilmer checked out gear to the thirteen football players coming out for wrestling. Because Lori always reminded her husband of what his father told him regarding people being more important than the work, he insisted they take a week off. Tom knew they needed the break. Even though he gave them a week, they surfaced two or three days later. They appreciated the time off and the chance to hang out after school with girlfriends.

Nearly every girl in the school wished to be Drew's girl, but he had not dated since his dad's death. Krissy Kinsley was his steady girlfriend since his freshman year but Drew withdrew from his relationships after the accident happened. With his father's memory, Drew focused on his athletic training and slowly rebuilt his friendships with his teammates over the summer. However, Drew's relationship with Krissy was far closer than he had realized or could explain. Every time he considered reaching back out to her, he felt the agony of losing his father. Subconsciously he was afraid if he reconnected with Krissy, he could lose her and feel that pain again. It became easier to avoid her than talk to her.

Drew took the entire week off from wrestling for a college visit scheduled with his mother. Before the week was over, his teammates headed to wrestling practice as the girls returned to their routines. Without the football players in the practice room for the first few days, Tom and Assistant Coach Hall, had more time to connect with the new kids in the room.

Pete Kirkpatrick, a junior football player, turned out on the first day of practice. Pete played guard on the football team at one hundred eighty pounds. He worried about making the varsity line-up with Drew and Charlie in the line-up. Charlie weighed one hundred seventy pounds, and Pete hoped Charlie would drop to the 155-pound class. If Charlie wrestled at 167-pounds and Drew dropped to 185-pounds, Pete knew he couldn't beat either of them out, and he'd be back on the junior varsity team. He contemplated not wrestling but didn't want to embarrass his family or to feel the shame from both sides of his relatives. So, Pete decided to report early to practice to gain a jump on his conditioning, and maybe it would work out. There was always next year. Besides, Pete did not have a girlfriend to hang out with after school.

The high schooler provided his own workout clothes, and they usually were a hodgepodge. Most of the wrestlers wore grey cotton sweatpants with various colored gym shorts pulled over them. Some wrestlers wore knee pads pulled over their sweatpants. Wrestling shoes were required. They were a simple high-top design, a soft, light shoe with a thin, flexible sole, and no metal eyelets which might cut the mat. They were either black or white and needed to be specially ordered through the coaches. Purchasing wrestling shoes was an expense most wrestlers, especially the younger ones, struggled to meet. Coach Kilmer and previous coaches collected shoes from graduating wrestlers and alumni and encouraged wrestlers who acquired new pairs to donate their old ones.

All they owned was one pair of sweatpants and maybe a couple of workout t-shirts, so most of them just hung their gear in their lockers and hoped the clothes dried out before the next practice. Their practice gear will be soaked with sweat way before practice ended due to their hard work, and the thermostat set near 80 degrees in the room. Sometimes their workout gear landed in a pile on the bottom of their metal locker and did not dry out overnight. Watching a wrestler putting on a cold, old t-shirt still dredged in perspiration made most people cringe. The foul odor of sweat lingered in the locker room and the wrestling room all season, prompting students in physical education classes and members of the basketball teams to complain to each other. Because of the status of the wrestling program at Cresco High School, no one dared speak a word to anyone in authority.

The coaches tried to model healthy hygiene for their wrestlers by wearing clean gear each day. They encouraged each individual to take their gear home at the end of every practice, but it did not happen for other than three or four athletes. Many of them lugged their gear home weekly, and a few just took their gear home only a couple of times during the whole season. Jose carried his gear home to the farm every night. His mother hand-washed the items in the kitchen sink with a bar of soap. She then draped them up to dry on a makeshift clothesline made with braided farm twine stretched between two chairs in their front room.

Assistant Coach Hall began helping with Spartan wrestling seventeen years earlier. When he came to Cresco in 1953, he applied to be the high school junior varsity basketball coach but got overlooked for a rookie teacher with far fewer credentials. The head basketball coach, who bypassed him, approached Joe to recruit him to volunteer with the basketball program. The basketball coach's audacity to ask him to coach without being paid outraged Joe so much that he volunteered to be involved with the wrestling program despite the fact of never having wrestled in his life.

He took the opportunity to learn from Coach Flannigan and developed into a more-than-adequate technician, a detailed instructor, and a terrific motivator. A year later, Coach Flannigan hired Joe to be a junior high wrestling coach and later made him his assistant high school coach.

Community members thought of Joe as "Mr.

Cresco" because of his dedication to service clubs and his church. Joe fries hamburgers in the Assumption Church food booth at the Howard County Fair in June and the school boosters' concessions during football games in the fall. He helps the Boy Scouts sell Christmas trees and seldom misses a Kiwanis Club, the Lions Club, or the Wildlife Club meetings.

Nearing forty, Joe, with his barrel chest, remains a robust, physical specimen but exhibited signs of aging. With his hairline well receded and a growing bald spot in the back of his head, he chose to have his long curly 1960s style brown locks clipped tight to a butch cut. Joe considered himself to be on the pudgy side for most of his adult life, but now he was quite aware of his belly extending over his expanded beltline.

As the assistant coach, boosters encouraged him to apply for the head position, but he decided against it. He never spoke it to anyone, but he based a portion of his decision on his knowledge of the team's lack of experience. He contemplated going back to coaching at the junior high school, but he knew the high school wrestlers needed support through the coaching transition to Tom.

Being over ten years older than Tom Kilmer, Coach Joe Hall experienced some reservations about continuing as an assistant, but he validated his decision after meeting Tom. Joe acknowledged Tom as an excellent communicator and an honest listener. In turn, Tom much appreciated Joe's tutelage regarding the significant wrestling tradition in Cresco and Joe's understanding of the school district's expectations and processes. Joe introduced the new head coach to the community's crucial wrestling boosters and provided incredible insight into each wrestler's personality in and out of the wrestling room. They spent time before the season collaborating over the Spartan program's requirements, including the schedule, practice plans, and coaching duties. Overseeing the start of practice and the conditioning at the end became Joe's responsibility.

They established terrific chemistry when working with their student-athletes and developed a remarkably close friendship in and out of school. As an avid trout fisherman, Joe fortified their relationship by sharing his "secret" trout fishing spots with Tom. The difficulty of Tom's first season bonded the pair even tighter.

Coach Hall continued to check out the headgear to each participant. Kids were busy in the room adjusting straps, snapping them on, and then taking them off to make more modifications. Wrestlers were required to wear headgear in matches. It has two padded metal ear covers held together with two straps over the top of the head and two straps around the back of the head. A chin strap kept it all in place. The ears get beat up terribly while wrestling if not protected, and the cartilage in the ear, when smacked, will break away from the skin, causing the blood and fluids to build up inside it. The ear would appear deformed with knots and bumps like cauliflower, resulting in it being called 'Cauliflower Ear.' If cauliflower ear swelled up too much, it became painful, and it required wrestlers to go to a doctor to drain the fluid. Cartilage damaged to a profound degree might leave the wrestler's ear with a permanent crinkled appearance.

Coach Kilmer required his athletes to wear their headgear in practice. Most of the boys complied, but his seniors did not wear them during practice in his first year. The coach absorbed the challenge to him as the new head of the program and let the defiance go, and only one boy developed a minor case of cauliflower ear. He did not say 'I told you so' because he knew it would be futile as the kid wore his cauliflower ear with pride and grit.

Unlike any other sport, a wrestling coach participates physically in all aspects of the practice, demonstrating techniques, teaching moves, and wrestling live with team members. Practice started with stretching with the usual arms, ankles, legs, and hips, plus extended time on the neck. Coach Hall incorporated the returning lettermen to lead the stretching. Wrestlers bridged by laying on their backs, arching up on their toes and the top of their heads, forming a 'bridge.' They rolled around on the heads, stretching out and strengthening the muscles in their necks. The highly flexible grappler rolled from ear to ear and then rocked fully forward to touch his nose to the mat.

After stretches, Coach Hall directed what he called shadow wrestling drills by going through different moves and series without an opponent to warm up and polish their methods. He shouted out, "long sit out, short sit, stand-up" or "inside leg-stand-up, turn in, high crotch" or "outside leg-stand-up, turn in, fireman's," and the wrestler went through the moves. A good drill, but at times Joe snickered to himself as he watched what appeared to be like an uncoordinated and out-of-sync ballerina troupe.

Coach Kilmer usually took over to demonstrate or refine a technique while Coach Hall moved throughout the room, helping individuals polish their moves. Coach Kilmer designed a specific four-day cycle to his practice schedule he learned from his college mentor. The neutral position and takedowns highlighted day one. Day two scheduled stand-ups and bottom position work. In contrast, the third day addressed the top position with breakdowns and pinning combinations. A focus on defensive and counter moves for the bottom and top positions took place on the fourth day.

Practices always included live wrestling in groups of three or four of the same weight. One wrestler took on the other group members one at a time for fifteen to sixty-second bursts starting in predetermined positions and executing a specific technique. The group numbered off, and the coaches announced, "1 versus 2," followed by "1 versus 3," and then "1 versus 4." After competing against every member of the group, the number two wrestler would do the same. Besides improving skills, live wrestling improved the stamina needed for matches. Takedowns, positioning, and takedown counters were addressed again towards the end of every practice as grapplers worked in pairs.

After Coach Hall led cool-down stretches, he checked the clock and enthusiastically called out, "I think it's time for…" and the entire crew shouted out, "Running!" If Coach did not think he heard enough excitement, he sounded off, "Holy moly, I did not hear you. I think it's time for…" "RUNNING!" When Coach Hall received the response he required, the wrestler changed into their running shoes, if they owned any, and headed to the hallway and stairs for additional conditioning work. Once the dual meet season began, practice intensity would change up and down as the coaches evaluated the team's needs. Practices ended with the squad huddling around Coach Hall.

"Spartans on three. 1,2,3!"

Forty-plus sweaty, stinky bodies roared, "SPARTANS!"

The detailed schedule ended precisely, so kids from the outlying communities and farm kids could catch the school district's activity buses home. At times, wrestlers drifted back into the wrestling room after conditioning to work on specific moves or keep a sweat going to lose weight.

The rest of the football players rolled into practice on Thursday except for Drew Parker.

CHAPTER 9

NEBRASKA

Saving his best football for his senior year, Drew led the Spartans to a six win season and was named to the all-state team on both offense and defense. The recruiting calls and mailings came flowing in from all across the country. Nebraska Head Coach Devaney's invitation to visit the university in Lincoln would be the only recruiting trip Drew accepted for the time being. Wishing to stay close to his mother but still play Division I football, he narrowed his other choices down to the University of Minnesota, Iowa State University, and the University of Wisconsin. He and his mother decided to wait on the outcome of his Nebraska trip before setting up other visits.

Drew and his mother headed to Lincoln, Nebraska, on Thursday. On Friday, they planned to meet with the college admissions recruiter, tour the campus, meet the football coaching staff and do a workout with some players and assistant coaches. Drew was overly excited with the opportunity to

105

watch Nebraska play the Oklahoma State Cowboys from the sidelines on Saturday afternoon. He would meet one more time with coaches before returning to Cresco on Sunday.

It appeared most people in Cresco shared Drew's excitement, well, almost all. A few Iowa State Cyclone fans and Iowa Hawkeye fans in town preferred to see him the following year in cardinal and gold or black and gold. The Iowa Hawkeyes were in a terrible mess, winning only one game the previous season. The Cyclones were up and coming under Coach Johnny Majors and were feverishly recruiting Drew, but Iowa State was nowhere close to the University of Nebraska's lure. The Corn Huskers, Big Eight Conference football champions and crowned NCAA national champions for two straight years, were attempting to become the first football program to win three national titles in a row.

Drew traveled on this visit with mixed emotions without his father, an enormous Nebraska "Big Red" fan. Drew's dad grew up in Shenandoah, Iowa, near the Missouri River and not far from Lincoln, Nebraska. The thought of the trip made Drew a little anxious and a little worried. He felt a dream coming true for him with the opportunity to meet Coach Devaney in person. They had conversations on the phone but yet to meet face to face. Official signing day was coming in February, but after he completes a workout on Friday with some of the assistant coaches, Drew expected to know by Sunday Nebraska's intent to sign him.

Sunday evening, Lori and Tom sat at their dining room table, completing their dinner by sharing the German chocolate cake the neighbor brought over, when unexpectedly, the doorbell rang. Tom moved to the door while his wife cleared the table.

They opened the door as Drew asked to come in. "I want to tell you 'bout my trip!"

"Awesome! We were just wondering if you were home. Glad you came by," Tom gave Drew a man hug, patting him on the back.

Drew began babbling as he entered, "It was incredible! The game, my gosh, the game was so much fun. Can you believe I stood on the sideline at Memorial Stadium watching NEBRASKA pound Oklahoma State 34-0? Jeez, they took me into the locker room. They are building a new locker room and a new weight room in the stadium opening next summer. It's huge! My gosh, Coach, the weight room is going to be as big as our gym!"

He kept going on as Lori helped him out of his letterman's jacket and hung it up on the coat rack. Taking his jacket off, Drew proudly displayed his new red t-shirt with white letters stating Nebraska Cornhuskers 1971 NCAA National Football Champions. They moved to the dining room and gathered around the dining room table. Lori placed a plate with cake and a fork in front of Drew.

Drew ignored the cake and kept babbling on, "I MET COACH BOB DEVANEY! Can you imagine? I shook Johnny Rodgers's hand! Do you know he should win the Heisman Trophy this year? Man, they call him The Jet! Boy, is he fast. He returned a punt 70 yards for a touchdown, and no one touched him. And I met their All-Americans Willie Harper and Rich Glover! Gosh, they're gigantic guys!"

"I got to eat lunch Friday with Joe Blahak. He plays cornerback, All-Big Eight, last year. You know, I am an inch taller and ten pounds heavier than he is, and he's probably going to be an All-American this year and be drafted by the pros. What a Stud! They're interested in me playing his position. He told me what it's like to play college football at Nebraska. All the fun they have and the traveling they do. What a great experience! And he's from a small town in Nebraska. Wow, they have over a hundred guys on the roster!"

"It sounds wonderful, but what did your mother think?" Lori interjected.

"Oh, Mrs. Kilmer, you'd be so proud of my mom. We sat in a conference room Saturday after the game with the assistant head coach, the defensive coordinator, and the defensive backs coach. I don't remember his name, but he's the guy telling us all the new NCAA rules starting next year, cutting the number of football scholarships they can offer so they can give athletic scholarships to girls for swimming, softball, or field hockey, because of

Title something."

"Title nine." This time her interruption caused Tom to roll his eyes at her.

"Mom goes…, excuse me, but what I think I hear you saying is WOMEN don't deserve sports scholarships or are you saying you don't have a scholarship for my son? Or maybe it's both."

Lori chimed in, "Good for her!"

Perturbed with his spouse for interrupting again, he gave her the old 'stink eye' before turning attention back to Drew, "What happened?"

"Well…" looking more at Lori than Tom, Drew continued, "The assistant coach stood up and said that's not true, they believe women deserve scholarships, AND they're making a verbal commitment to me for a full ride to the University of Nebraska to play football!"

Both Lori and Tom leaped up and grabbed Drew and embraced him. Lori screeched, "You're going to Nebraska!"

Suddenly she pushed away and glared at him, "Oh, no, wait, what…what did you tell them?"

"Of course, I said yes. It's what Dad and I hoped for. But it's not official until signing day in February. So, it's kind of an official unofficial offer."

Surprisingly, Drew turned subdued. "There's an issue, Coach. They gave me a weight training program and diet they want me to follow to beef up. There's no way I can do this and cut seventeen pounds to get to 185."

"Oh, shoot," Tom muttered.

Lori glanced at her husband out the corner of her eye and prompted him with a high pitch squeal, "People are more important than the work."

"I know," rolled his eyes again as he sarcastically replied, "but thanks for the reminder, Honey." Tom paused and took a deep breath. "It's okay if you don't come out for wrestling. We'll still be here for you."

"Whoa, I AM coming out for wrestling. In fact, the Nebraska coaches encourage their recruits to play basketball or wrestle. It's... I won't be in the line-up. I cannot cut the weight to 185, doing what Nebraska wants me to do with the weights and food. I won't challenge Hoss at heavyweight. I have my sport, and this is his." Drew held up three fingers with his left hand as if doing the Boy Scout salute and covered his heart with his right hand. "I promise, if you let me, to work hard every day and make Hoss, Pete, and Charlie better."

"You betcha!" Coach snapped a military salute back at him, and they laughed.

"Thanks, Coach. I wasn't sure what I expected you to say, but I shoulda known," Drew and Coach man-hugged one more time, patting each other on the back. "I told Mom I wouldn't be long, so I better get home. See you tomorrow, AT practice!"

Lori retrieved Drew's jacket, helped him put it on, and hugged him one more time. "Good night,

Drew. Congratulations! Your father would be so proud of you. We love you."

"I know, and thanks for everything."

"Night, Drew."

The duo stood in the open doorway until Drew pulled away from the curb. They waved goodbye and stepped inside. Tom shut the door behind them. Tom, with half a frown, tried to hide his disappointment, "Shoot, maybe I should take him fishing."

Lori kissed him on his cheek.

CHAPTER 10

SEASON

The first meet of the year brought out excitement with the issuing of uniforms at the end of practice the day before. A few years earlier, the Iowa State High School Athletic Association modified the uniform requirements allowing the newer designed one-piece singlets to be worn with or without tights. Wrestling programs state-wide began transitioning to the singlets.

When it came to replacing uniforms, high schools were not much different than a big farm family with 'hand-me-down' clothes. The old varsity uniforms moved to the junior-varsity team as coaches passed junior-varsity uniforms on to the C-team or junior high school team. The Cresco High School athletic department budgeted new singlets for the varsity wrestling team, and the uniform shuffle began.

Many of the younger athletes felt the awkwardness of wearing a singlet that seemed to

113

highlight 'everything' specifically their private parts, and they were relieved to be issued the old three-piece uniforms. The three pieces included a snug-fitting tank top with extended tails wrapping through the crotch and buttoning in the front. Tights with stirrups hooked under the wrestler's heels as they pulled them up to the waist. A pair of trunks over the top of the tights provided the young wrestler with another layer of protection from revealing any embarrassing outline of their 'junk.'

The varsity wrestlers were excited about their new blue singlets with a large white 'C' on the chest and their issued matching new blue tights to wear underneath the singlet if they chose. Because they had always worn tights, most starters selected to wear them under their singlets, except for Bingo and Charlie. Bingo felt hot and sweaty in his tights, especially during all-day tournaments, and became comfortable without them, while Charlie said, "The girls need to know what they're missing!"

Each varsity wrestler had a blue custom hooded pull-over warm-up top. Embroidered on the front was 'Cresco Spartan Wrestling' in white lettering outlined in black. Individual weight classes were printed on the back of the warm-ups.

Perennial powerhouse West Waterloo presented a formidable obstacle for the Spartan's first meet of the season. The Cresco fans crammed the gymnasium to see how the Spartans matched up against last year's state champions. At the end of the exhibition matches and the junior-varsity meet, the crowd stood as the pep band played the school fight song "Go Cresco High School" and the varsity trotted out into the gym. A Spartan tradition continued as they jogged the perimeter of the mat circle twice as the song continued. Settling down on the edge of the mat in front of the team chairs, the wrestlers lined up by their weight classifications, lightest to heaviest. Individually, they went through their stretching exercises.

The elementary and junior high boys in the gym bleachers dreamed of being on the gym floor wearing the Spartan varsity warm-up uniform and going through the routine. They watched the cheerleaders assemble behind Cresco's 98-pounder as he stretched. With pom-poms shaking above their heads, the cheer began, "Wes, Wes, he's our man. If he can't do it, Spider can!" The cheerleaders then leaped behind Spider and started the cheer again, "Spider, Spider, he's our man…" and so on, moving up the weight classes, sounding out individual starter's names one at a time. Finishing with Hoss at heavyweight, the cheerleaders concluded with, "if he can't do it, THE TEAM CAN!" As everyone clapped and yelled, the boys in the stands fantasized about being on the mat and having their names called out in the cheer.

The stretching ended when the referee requested the team captains from both teams to come to the center of the mat to determine which

115

wrestler would have their choice of position to begin the second period. With a flip of a coin, one team would get the option of the odd-numbered or even-numbered matches for their team's choice. Following this lackluster ceremony, the captains would return to the sideline, and the first match of the dual meet would begin.

When the Kilmers came to town, they immediately began attending school activities to support students and the community. They noticed right away that one of Lori's clients was attending home athletic events. Brady McKane was a young man in his late teens with Down Syndrome. Most kids with Down Syndrome were kept isolated at home, but Brady's parents felt it was vital for him to be involved in the community and to help the community accept people with the disorder. Though his parents persistently tried to encourage others to interact with Brady, he sat by himself at the edge of the student section during football and volleyball games with little or no contact with anyone. He loved watching the Spartans and reveled in being around the student body, so they kept bringing him to activities. By the time the wrestling season started, Lori had an idea to include Brady in the wrestling meets and suggested it to him, his parents, and her husband.

Incorporating Lori's suggestion, Tom had his captains, instead of returning directly to the team chairs, walk over to Brady and slap five on his hands.

Then they exchange high-fives with junior high and elementary students before returning to the team's bench area. By the time Coach's second season rolled around, the small gesture had evolved into an opening gala. With the completion of the coin flip, a very confident Brady, now sitting in the middle of the front row of the student section, stood tall as the captains came towards him. He turned towards the bleachers and 'shhh'-ed everyone by putting an index finger to his lips. The crowd responded by becoming entirely quiet, waiting in anticipation of his next move. The Spartan captains slapped their now customary fives on Brady's outreached hands. He hesitated for a second, and then he quickly shot both fists into the air. The crowd, adults and students, roared, "CRESCO!" and launched into high-fiving each other. Dozens of students reached down or came out of the stands to give Brady a high-five or ten. Brady beamed in the spotlight.

Bob Siddens helped built a wrestling dynasty at West Waterloo High School. The Wahawks' most famous alumni, Dan Gable, coached by Siddens, went undefeated in high school and won a gold medal in the Munich Olympics a few months earlier, adding to the lore of West Waterloo wrestling. The defending state champions rolled into Cresco with another strong, intimidating line-up. Coach Siddens already had his team in mid-season form for the first dual meet of the year. They graduated both of their previous state champions and established a veteran competitor at nearly every weight class, including two returning state medalists and two other state qualifiers. The only freshman in their line-up weighed in at the 98-pound class, and he over-powered Wes for a fall. Charlie wrestled at 167-pounds, and with no Drew in the line-up, Pete wrestled at 185. Both wrestlers expected easy matches but lost close decisions. Spider lost by a point at 105-pounds giving up a takedown at the final buzzer.

Jose surprised everyone in the stands by winning with a pin. It was his first match ever in competition, but no one knew it or suspected it. The referee raised Jose's hand with the match's completion, and Jose turned to the referee, "Gracias por arbitrary mi coinciden."

The referee calmly followed Jose over to the Spartan coaches, appearing puzzled, "Your kid just spoke to me in Spanish. What the heck did he say?"

Coach Kilmer reacted with a clueless shrug and deferred to his assistant, who knew a little Spanish, "I believe he said, thank you for refereeing my match."

"Oh...umm, son of a gun, tell him he's welcome." A little shocked, the referee nodded at Jose and returned to the middle of the mat.

Rollie scored an escape with fifteen seconds left to break a tied score and salvage a victory at 132-pounds. Bing followed up with a fall in the third period after cruising to an 8-2 lead but seemed exhausted at the match's end. No one else came close to winning a match. Hoss vastly underestimated the junior West Waterloo heavyweight, who went undefeated as a junior varsity wrestler the previous season when he wrestled behind a senior state champion. Out of position the entire match, Hoss got taken down to his back in the first period and ending up losing 10-4.

Expecting a better showing from the team, the disappointed crowd solemnly exited the gymnasium at the end of the Spartans' 26-15 loss. Many diehard fans could be heard mumbling to each other about the coach and his team's preparation.

The Spartans came into the wrestling room Monday with their heads between their tails. Coach Kilmer addressed the squad, letting them know he takes responsibility for their loss to West Waterloo. "Listen, guys. We weren't ready for that team. I take all the responsibility. WE WILL get better, and WE WILL do it in a hurry. We will not see those guys again until state, and then we will take it to them. But we are going to have to work harder. Our conditioning isn't where it needs to be. We have to get better defensively on our feet. Alright... Get it?" The entire squad responded by shouting, "GOT IT!"

Coach Hall blew his whistle, "Line up for stretches!" Bing, Drew, and Hoss moved to the front of the room. As the seniors took the lead, Coach Hall

119

moved over to the head coach. They stood shoulder to shoulder at the side of the room. Not wanting anyone else to hear, the assistant softly spoke, "Holy cow, look at the size of the bruise on Spider's cheek. I don't remember him getting a head butt or anything. I know his match was a war, but..."

Coach Kilmer answered him, "I know. The Waterloo kid hammered him pretty hard. But Spider still shoulda beat him."

The Spartans won their next two dual meets and took third at a tournament in Eagle Grove before Christmas. Still, the team's intensity seemed lacking, frustrating Coach Kilmer and Coach Hall. The pair spent hours collaborating on the next steps to motivate the crew. Without Drew in the line-up and Bing not dominating his challengers as he usually does, the Spartans missed its leadership and needed someone to step up.

Weighing ninety-two pounds without cutting weight, an undersized Wes Sorenson didn't make it to the end of either dual meet matches, but the Spartans had no other alternative at 98-pounds. When Wes 'counted the lights' in his first three varsity matches, Coach Hall recognized a fragile and disintegrating confidence level in him. The assistant coach suggested that Coach Kilmer not take Wes to the rigid Eagle Grove tournament. The head coach respected his call and let Wes go to a junior varsity tournament instead to give him a little success.

Spider picked up dual meet wins at 105-

pounds and breezed to the tournament's finals before losing a 6-2 decision. Coach Kilmer's 112 and 119 pounders won two dual meet matches, and they both won two and lost two matches in their first tournament of the year.

Jose easily won two more dual matches on his way to the tournament finals. Behind 3-2 starting the third period, Coach Kilmer's strategy directed Jose's choice of the down position. The coach felt confident Jose would easily escape, then work for a takedown to win, but it did not happen. Jose barely moved underneath, being ridden for the entire period, losing the match. Coach shook his head in disappointment. Second-guessing himself, Tom thought maybe he should have adjusted the strategy by having Jose choosing the neutral position to begin the third period.

Bing effortlessly won his dual meet matches at 138, building lofty leads and then riding his opponents out. Without any attempt at cutting more weight, he stepped on the scale at one hundred thirty-two pounds during weigh-ins at the Eagle Grove Tournament, surprising himself and both coaches. Coach flip-flopped Bing and Rollie for the tournament and entered Bing at 132, where he became the number one seed and cruised to the finals, but Bing got a bloody nose in the finals. They could not stop the bleeding within the injury time allotment and forfeited the championship match after leading 4-0. Rollie rolled two dual meet victories at 132-pounds and placed third at 138-pounds in the tournament.

The Spartan line-up had yet settled in at 145 and 155-pounds, allowing the coach the opportunity to insert different wrestlers into the varsity line-up. The team picked up two victories in the dual meet matches at 155-pounds, split the decisions at 145-pounds, and then added two fourth-place tournament finishes.

Charlie appeared content to wrestle at 167-pounds, picked up two dual meet wins, and took a disappointing third in the tournament. Pete won one and lost one in the duals, ended up on his back during a scramble situation, and was pinned in the 185-pound finals at Eagle Grove.

Two schools invited to the Eagle Grove Tournament did not field a heavyweight contestant, so Drew Parker participated as an unattached entry, not scoring any team points. Drew weighed in at two hundred and three pounds while the rest of the heavyweight field weighed two hundred forty pounds or more. Hoss Erickson bolstered his nickname by tipping the scale at two hundred seventy-six pounds. The highlight of the tournament for Cresco was having both Hoss and Drew reaching the finals by pins. Drew forfeited the title match to Hoss, the only Spartan to bring home the first-place medal. It felt so satisfying for Drew just to compete. However, answering all the other coaches' questions regarding Drew Parker started to wear on the head coach.

Jose continued to thank referees in Spanish at the end of his matches throughout the entire season. The coaching duo agreed that Jose's expression of gratitude was admirable but pressed Jose on why he chose to speak Spanish, not English, to the refs.

Jose replied, "My mamá told me I must thank the judge when I end my bouts, no matter I win or lose. To honor Mamá, I thank them in Spanish, gracias. I hope they understand. When I get home after a match, she does not ask me how I did. She only asks me if I thanked the judge." Jose paused and enthusiastically went on, "Papá says nothing but waits 'til Mamá is not looking. He raises his eyebrows and looks my way. I shake my head yes or no. If yes, he grins... 'til Mamá turns around."

The word of Jose's gratitude spread throughout the Northeast Iowa Referees Association, so it needed little explanation in future dual meets. Tournaments and matches outside the northeast Iowa region were a different story. The Spartan coaches tried to give the referees a heads-up, but Jose's remarks still mystified some referees. Once they understood, they appreciated his respectful attitude. One ref caught Jose off guard, nearly making him smile, when he answered Jose, "Con mucho gusto," meaning "my pleasure."

CHAPTER 11

BLIZZARD

Winter arrived early, not necessarily by the time of year, but by the storm's ferociousness. The wrestling team returned to Cresco late Saturday night from the Eagle Grove tournament. A majority of the wrestlers rode home from Eagle Grove with their parents. The cheerleaders and four Spartans joined the two coaches on the school bus for the one hundred-twenty-mile trip to Cresco. The two-and-a-half-hour ride gradually turned into a three-hour journey as the school bus driver drove the last fifteen miles cautiously through blowing and drifting snow. The bus arrived at the high school a few minutes before midnight but well ahead of the snowstorm's significant impact.

Tom and Joe remained at school to make sure each wrestler and cheerleader made it home safely by requiring them to call the coaches when they arrived at their residences. When they were sure everyone successfully landed at their destinations, the coaches parted ways. Tom took Spider across town and dropped him off at his house before heading to his own home. The snow continued to come down, making it difficult to see the road through his headlights in the darkness of the night. The wind polished the streets to an icy sheet and intermittently left streaks of snowdrifts varying in heights and widths.

Thankful for not competing with other vehicles, Tom carefully managed his way through the treacherous streets and down his alley to park his car in his garage. It was nearly two in the morning when he crawled under the blankets next to his sleeping wife. Lori scarcely stirred and murmured, "Sheesh, your feet are cold!" and rolled over away from Tom.

Sunday mornings at the Kilmers typically found the twosome dividing up the Des Moines Register at the dining room table as they attended to their morning coffee and waited to leave for church. Tom typically claimed the sports pages, checked for wrestling scores and other sporting news, and then moved on to the funny papers. Meanwhile, Lori would collect the front page news and the entertainment section. But there would be no newspaper or church this Sunday morning.

Silently Lori had slipped out of bed early and glided down the stairs letting Tom sleep in after his long day and late night. Surprised by the time, Tom rolled out of bed close to ten o'clock. By then, the storm had become a full-on blizzard with wind gusts over forty miles per hour. The wind howled as he followed his regular bathroom routines. He changed out of his shorts and the t-shirt he slept in, and he outfitted himself in his red Iowa State Cyclone workout attire. Putting on a pair of wool socks, the coach dragged himself down the stairs to see his wife. The smell of coffee filled the air as he reached the landing. He continued down the three steps bottoming out in the living room.

Lori, snuggled up in a blanket and reading a book, sat on the couch with her back to the stairs. In hearing her husband's heavy steps lumbering down the stairs, she finished reading the page, took the bookmark from the end of her book, and moved it to the page she just completed. The purple bookmark was a Valentine's Day gift from her husband and had red hearts and the Bible verses from First Corinthians thirteen printed on it. "What is Love?" was their anthem. He read the verses to her at their wedding, and he reread the verses to her every Valentine's Day and anniversary. He had difficulty reading it out loud to Lori without tearing up, especially when she began crying.

Lori closed her book and leaned her head back over the top of the couch. "Good morning, Sweety. Good tournament?"

Bending over the top of her, Tom gave her an upside-down kiss, "Good morning to you. We did okay. I'll tell you all about it in a bit. How much snow did we get?"

"The Cresco radio reported eight inches, and we are supposed to get four more today. But the wind is closing all the roads."

With the snow coming down and the continual winds of thirty-five miles an hour, the blizzard created a white-out. Tom moved to the broad front window and gazed out. The wind made it appear it was snowing sideways down the street, and he could barely identify the outline of their neighbor's house across the way.

"Glad we beat this storm home last night. I would have hated being stuck somewhere between here and Eagle Grove. We would've been there a while. How cold is it?"

Lori had opened her book back up, paused, and answered, "twenty-one degrees when I came downstairs this morning. The radio said the low overnight had been seventeen degrees with a wind chill of negative four. Check the thermometer, see what it is now. There's a new pot of coffee brewing just for you."

"Thanks."

Tom caressed Lori's shoulder as he passed by her on his way to the kitchen and then across to the back door leading out to the closed-in porch in an attempt to verify the temperature. The previous tenant had hung a thermometer on a metal bracket outside one of the back windows swiveled to read it from inside the porch. A quick peek out the kitchen door window into the porch area revealed a layer of an inch or more of white snow on the floor, which the strong winds had blown in through the cracks around the window frames and door frames. In his stocking feet, Tom decided he didn't need to know the exact temperature, and twenty-one degrees sufficed.

Peering through the porch and out one of its back windows, he noticed a four-foot snow drift blocking the entry door to the detached garage. There would be plenty of shoveling to clear the garage's walkway and then more digging to clear the alleyway for their cars. The entire alley would be a neighborhood effort, but it would be fruitless to begin until the wind stopped blowing.

He called out to his wife as he kept staring out the window, "Where did we leave the shovel?"

"I'm sure it's hanging up in the garage."

"Dang," he muttered to himself, then responded to his spouse. "Yeah, I was afraid of that."

He turned his attention to the coffee pot and retrieved his favorite cup off the open shelf next to the refrigerator. He paused, wistfully gazing at the two dozen coffee cups of various sizes and colors representing relationships with his friends, relatives, students, and wrestlers. He had a few more cups on his desk at school. The cups carried messages of appreciation, honor, and humor connected to teaching, coaching, or fishing, such as

129

"Best Teacher Ever," "Have no fear, the wrestling coach is here!", and "A bad day of fishing is better than a good day of work." Each cup prompted a personal story or two, which Tom enthusiastically shared with guests.

One of the cups held a special place of honor in the midpoint of the front row. Tom's father bought the cup for him when Tom was eleven years old. Stopping at the Lake Mille Lacs Fishing Shop to purchase bait during one of their winter fishing expeditions, Tom became fascinated with the arrangement of coffee cups next to the cash register.

A picture of a weathered ice fishing shack sitting on the snow and ice-covered lake blazed the side of the white coffee cup. Snow drifts lay against the rustic building's plank walls, with a wooden Lake Mille Lacs sign hanging at a slant over the shack's door. The words "Life Doesn't Get Better Than This" was printed under the picture. The youngster was sure the shed pictured on the cup was the one they were renting for their fishing excursion, even though the hundreds of ice sheds on the lake appeared the same. A painted ceramic walleye fish formed the handle of the cup. Another but smaller ceramic walleye leaped off the bottom rim inside the cup. The fish appeared when the cup was half empty, and then it began to emerge like a fish jumping up out of the water.

Years later, while Tom showed it off to a

colleague, the fish handle broke when his friend accidentally dropped it back down on the desk. Tom carefully glued it back on. Safeguarding it, he kept the cup at home and seldomly used it, but he still displayed it in distinction and awaited the opportunity to share his father's stories.

Two cups had been given to him by a female student he had in his physical education class during her junior and senior years when he taught at Cooper High School. Tom knew the challenge of teaching in a required PE class with students with limited skills or athletic ability who did not like or, in this girl's words, "Hate PE." Tom acknowledged her effort in his class and rewarded her for her improvement, but even more significantly, he admired her spunk, intelligence, and willingness to engage him in conversation.

Every day she initiated a conversation with Tom, "What are we doing today, Mr. Kilmer? Does it have anything to do with running or a ball?"

"Don't worry, you will love it!" Tom always answered.

The girl always shook her head no and replied, "Not a chance."

Though their interests differed considerably, they both possessed a keen sense of humor, which helped them develop a healthy teacher-student friendship. The young lady gave him coffee cups for presents at Christmas time both years she attended his class. The first one had a message reading, "Who

131

is Jim Teacher?" Over the school year, she discovered Mr. Kilmer's interests and selected a second cup's message reading, "Education is Important, Fishing is Importanter!"

She graduated valedictorian of her class and received an academic scholarship to Mankato State College with a letter of recommendation from her physical education teacher.

The Natvig family presented another cup to the coach. Early last summer, on a fishing morning at the Natvig farm, Tom arrived without the customary greeting from Lynette at the back porch. He discovered Bill, Lynette, and Bing, uncharacteristically seated at the kitchen table and eating breakfast when he arrived. They tried hard to remain preoccupied as they welcomed Tom. He sensed something was up as he sat down in his designated chair, noticing the new cup out of the corner of his eye. The Natvig clan knew Tom's morning ritual of beginning with a cup of coffee before he ate his breakfast. They had the special cup already filled with coffee, sitting in front of his place setting. The trio tried not to stare at him, and he tried not to gaze at the coffee cup.

Intentionally ignoring the cup, Tom engaged the threesome in small-talk describing the weather forecast as he served himself fried bacon, potatoes, and eggs off of the platter in the center of the table and commenced eating. The conversation went quiet until Lynette's patience ran out. "For Pete's sake, Tom, would you PLEASE drink your coffee!"

Tom burst into laughter, followed by the group. The four other Natvig children had hurried to finish their chores and leapfrogged their way back into the kitchen to be in on Coach's reaction to his gift.

The youngsters surrounded him as he read the cup out loud, "Nice fish you caught, do you mind if I use it for bait?" Tom raised the cup in the air and sarcastically stated, "Not funny, not funny at all! Who's responsible for getting me this cup?"

He tried to appear angry as he stared down each of the younger siblings. At first, they hesitated and looked at their big brother out the corners of their eyes, expecting him to bail them out. But then they saw through the coach's façade and kept giggling.

Unable to stop laughing, Bingo confessed to finding the cup in Eddie's Sporting Goods Store in Decorah over the weekend. "Coach, ya know, if the shoe fits!"

The snow and wind whistling outside brought Tom out of his daydream and back to his kitchen. As he poured his coffee, he continued to stare out the window at the storm, fully aware of how the snow and cold affected his wrestlers' lives. The blizzard would force his farm boys to be up earlier than usual and be out in the cold weather throughout the day to ensure their livestock's and livelihood's safety. The milking schedules took place for the dairy farmers no matter the weather. Still, the blizzard presented a different concern for the dairy farmers with their milk haulers' ability to access their farms to transport the milk to the Cresco Creamery.

Spider's father would take the opportunity to earn some cash by working the day and into the late night, using a friend's tractor with a front loader to remove snow from driveways. A pint of whiskey in the tractor cab would help keep him warm. It would not surprise Tom to know that Spider and his mother would gather in their warm kitchen baking cookies and playing cards and board games away from the coldness of the rest of the house. They will leave the cupboard doors under the sinks in the kitchen and bathroom open throughout the day and night and let the water run a trickle to prevent pipes from freezing. Later in the day, Spider will venture out to shovel the sidewalks and driveway and then help his neighbors. The extra blankets and quilts stacked deep on the beds provided each of them a warm night's sleep once they passed the initial chill.

His wrestlers didn't know any differently, and their gritty attitude towards their survival contributed substantially to their mental toughness on the wrestling mat.

Tom returned to his task. Ironically, his favorite cup related directly to his responsiveness. His intuitive wife had given him the red cup with a subtle message scripted in white, "Sorry I wasn't listening. I was thinking about fishing." Tom recognized himself in this quote, privately confessing his guilt with other ideas, people, or events, wrestling or fishing being on his mind when he needed to focus his attention. This cup was a friendly reminder to him to give his full attention to the people he interacts with, especially the people he loves. Filling his cup, Tom smiled to himself, setting the percolator back down on the counter. To warm his hands, he wrapped both of them, momentarily, around the mug. He took a sip as he peeked into the living room at his wonderful and beautiful wife cuddled up on the couch. With a slight Elvis rendition, Tom sang out, "Hey, Honey, have I told you lately that I love you?"

"How much?" she answered, accepting her role in the interaction.

Stepping back into the living room, "This much!" But he extended only his left arm out to the side with a cupped hand as if describing a big fish. But the other arm stayed at his waist, holding his coffee.

Knowing the routine, Lori acted confused, "Where's your other hand?"

"Oh, it's way down the street, Hun!"

Lori smiled. She loved playing the little game. Tom bent over and kissed her again before sitting down next to her.

CHAPTER 12

COLLAPSE

The following Thursday morning, right before Christmas break, Bing rolled out at his bed at 5:05 am and sat up feeling chilled from sweating. He turned his bedroom light on and noticed some dry blood on the back of his hand. Peering in the mirror, he spotted a smear of blood under his nose and on his cheek. His pillowcase showed a little two-inch oval of blood. He took the pillowcase and hustled to the bathroom to clean up before anybody noticed. He used a bar of soap to try to wash the pillowcase clean but had little success. Bing threw the pillowcase along with the t-shirt he wore to bed, into the clothes hamper, and then dressed for chores.

His mother was facing the stovetop, cooking breakfast, when he scampered through the kitchen. "Mornin', Mom."

"You're running late this morning, Deary," she peeked over her shoulder at him as he slipped out the kitchen door to the back porch. "Your dad is

137

still sleeping," she expressed before the door closed. Knowing Bingo could still hear her through the door, his mom continued but raised her voice a little louder, "He's been up at the chicken coop all night, making sure they have heat."

Bing heard her and promptly put on his black and red plaid wool chore jacket, tugged on his barn boots, and threw on a stocking cap and leather gloves. He ignored the cold even as he observed his breath inside the porch. He headed down the shoveled path cut out of the foot and half of snow covering the ground. With the temperature in the teens, the snow presented a crisp layer as it glistened in the moonlight, and Bing heard the crunch of the snow as he surefootedly hustled to the barn.

The temperature inside the barn ran ten to fifteen degrees warmer due to the body heat from the animals. Bing hung his jacket and cap on a hook inside the barn door. It took more effort than usual this morning to climb the ladder to the top of the hay bales, blaming it on the cold. He kicked two bales down the shoot and climbed back down. Carrying one bale of hay to the far end of the barn, Bing interacted with the cows, calling some of them by name, wishing them a good morning, or telling them to move out of the way as he broke up the bale into the feeder. Then he worked his way back to the other end of the barn, where he broke up the second bale and spread it into the other end of the feeder.

Bing picked up a five-gallon metal feed bucket, scooped corn from the corn bin, and distributed it to the cattle trough. He then did the same with a partial bucket of corn, dumping it into the hog trough in a separate pig pen at the other end of the barn. Ice formed over the cattle's water tank, so he shattered it with the wooden baseball bat brought out to the barn for just the purpose of breaking up ice sheets. Bing fetched fresh water for the pigs before grabbing the broad shovel and running it down the barn floor, pushing the cow manure to the back door leading into the feedlot. Too cold to hose it down because ice could build-up, causing the cattle to slip and be injured, so he ran the shovel two more times. The job would have to wait until it warmed up a bit later in the day. His father will use the tractor loader to move the manure pile from the barn to a heap on the edge of the feedlot. In the spring, they will pull a spreader behind the tractor using the manure to fertilize the pasture.

Bing's morning routine during the wrestling season did not vary more than a few minutes. Putting on his jacket and cap back on in the barn, he marched back to the porch, where he took off his boots and hung up his outer work gear. Then he scrambled up to his room and changed into his sweatpants, hoodie, and running shoes before loading up his school clothes into his backpack.

Following his run to the high school, he will shower and switch into his school attire in the locker room.

His dad arrived in the kitchen to a waiting cup of coffee. He was sitting in his familiar chair at the kitchen table when Bing reappeared. His siblings had rolled out of bed, and Bing heard his little sisters fighting in the bathroom over the toothpaste. Lynette poured Bing a half cup of coffee.

"We almost lost our chickens last night. Dang heater wasn't working right. I got up at 1:30 to check on it. Glad I did. I took the heater from the machine shed over and toasted them up. Fried chicken! Ha! Then I spent the rest of the night fixing the other one. I think everything is okay now. Sorry, I didn't get down to the barn to help you feed."

"Not a problem, Dad. Too cold to open the doors for cleaning, so I just pushed it to the end."

His dad replied, "I'll take care of it later."

Bing smiled as he downed his coffee, picked up a banana, peeled it, and started eating it. Checking the clock, he announced, "Gotta go!"

Bing's mother handed him a brown paper sack with an apple and fried ham sandwich for lunch. She told him to have a great day. He answered, "You, too!"

He heard his dad say, "See ya, son!" as he hesitated at the kitchen door to finish the banana and threw away the peel. Tucking his sack lunch in his backpack, Bing strapped the pack over his shoulders, pulled the hood up over his stocking cap, and tied the string tight under his chin. He used a towel to cover his mouth and tied it around the back of his head. Like the hundreds of other times, Bing put on his gloves and hopped out the back porch for his three-mile jog to school.

Robbie, one of the high school wrestler's little brother, delivered the daily issue of the Des Moines Register around the northeast side of Cresco each morning. Unless it was storming, he always rode his bicycle, even on snowy roadways.

He liked to meet Bing at the corner of Cemetery Road at seven forty, and then he rode his bike alongside him for two blocks before Bing turned right on 5th Avenue towards the high school. If Robbie beat Bing to the corner, he would see him coming down the road and ride to meet him. Sometimes their timing was perfect, and they met at the corner. If Bing had already passed the corner, he would pedal faster to catch up, saying "hi" to his hero. The twosome exchanged few words, but Robbie loved the idea of being next to the best wrestler in Cresco.

Robbie will never forget the one morning earlier in the fall when he failed to turn on his alarm. He hurried as fast as he could but still arrived nearly four minutes late at the meeting corner. Disappointment set in, knowing he was going to miss Bingo. But when Robbie arrived at the Cemetery Road corner, Bing was running around in circles in the middle of the intersection, waiting for

141

him. "Hey, afraid something happened to my buddy. Let's go!"

Robbie rode his bike next to Bing for six blocks, all the way to the high school, and then retraced his path to finish his paper route. He glowed all the way, reveling in being called Bing's "buddy."

On this Thursday morning, however, the paperboy arrived at the corner right at the usual meeting time but was unable to see Bingo in either direction. Disheartened in the darkness of the morning, he waited a minute or two and assumed Bing already went by. Robbie then returned to his paper delivery route. At the corner where Bing turns to the high school, the youngster squinted to see how far his hero had gotten.

Twenty feet in front of Robbie down 5th Avenue, he detected what appeared to be a small pile of dirty snow in the middle of the snow-packed street. Doing a double-take, he recognized Bing's backpack and raced towards the pile. Underneath the pack, Bing had collapsed in the center of the road. Robbie called his name as he hopped off his bicycle. He grabbed Bing, but there was no response. He shook him and checked his breathing without thinking. Searching around for help, Robbie rushed towards the nearest house with lights on, stumbling as he tried to hurdle the pile of snow the plows pushed up over the curb. Recovering his balance, Robbie raced to the front door, pounded on it as he rang the doorbell, and cried out for help.

Sandy Kinsley came to the door in her robe. The young paperboy kept screaming, "Help! Help! Bingo needs help! Hurry!" pointing to the middle of the street.

Sandy screeched at her husband to call for an ambulance. She raced out with Robbie to the small lump of grey sweats in the street. The whole town of Cresco woke up to the sound of an ambulance siren as it streaked across town.

Rushed to the Howard County Memorial Hospital, Bing regained consciousness. Dr. Coby ran a series of tests and had a strong suspicion, but the Cresco hospital's limited resources did not allow for the additional lab work needed for confirmation. The next day, the doctor sent Bing to the Mayo Clinic in Rochester, Minnesota, sixty-five miles north. Bing would be in good hands in one of the world's best hospitals.

School excused students at noon Thursday for Christmas vacation with no school on Friday. Christmas Day was the following Monday. Lori's family planned a holiday get-together at her brother's home in Owatonna, Minnesota, thirty minutes past Rochester. The couple intended to drive to Anoka on Thursday to see Tom's parents and then spend the weekend and Christmas Day in Owatonna.

They changed their plans and stayed in Cresco another night. Tom and Lori spent Thursday

143

evening at the hospital supporting Bing and doing what they could for his parents and siblings. Assistant Coach Hall made telephone calls ensuring neighbors took care of the Natvig's farm chores.

When the doctor decided to send him to the Mayo Clinic, the Kilmer pair packed up Friday morning and headed to Owatonna. Being in Owatonna, the couple would be thirty minutes closer to Rochester than Cresco, making it easier to visit Bingo on Saturday, Sunday, and again on Christmas Day afternoon. Tom called Coach Hall to keep him informed and have him run practice Tuesday morning if the Kilmers decided to stop at the hospital on their way back to Cresco. They were at the clinic on Tuesday with the Natvig family when the doctors gave them the diagnosis.

The pair drove the sixty miles to Cresco in the late afternoon without hardly uttering a word to each other. Coach Hall called all the wrestlers and asked them to come to a meeting that evening at the high school and bring their parents. They heard the urgency in Coach Hall's phone conversation, and nearly all the wrestlers, with at least one of their parents, assembled in the school cafeteria to hear Tom explain the emergency. He brought Lori and, on her suggestion, asked the high school counselor to attend for support.

"We all noticed Bing has not been the Bingo we have watched wrestle in the past. My goodness, he's a two-time state runner-up, and we expected him to be a state champ this year. Just an incredible wrestler with a heart of gold and great love for his family and teammates. You are aware he collapsed in the middle of the street as he jogged to school last Thursday morning. Doc Coby sent him to the Mayo Clinic. His family gave me permission to share with you his diagnosis, and it's not good, guys. Bing has acute myeloid leukemia."

His voice quivered as tears overtook him. He tilted his head back and closed his eyes. Coach Hall stepped up and took over. "I'm sure you've all heard of leukemia. What it is, is a cancer of the blood where abnormal cells take over the normal blood cells. But these abnormal cells do not fight off infections or carry oxygen like normal blood cells and other stuff. It is extremely aggressive."

A cracking voice hollered out, "Is he going to die?"

Tom regained his composure, took a deep breath, and tried to speak with an upbeat tone, "Untreated?... the answer might be a 'yes.' The doctors at Mayo have an amazingly effective treatment plan for him, and it's going to be tough going for a while. They are extremely optimistic, and we know what kind of fighter Bingo is."

But most people present sensed Tom's lack of optimism, and the room became awkwardly silent for a moment. Parents moved to be with their sons, and sons found their parents. Tears flowed from some while others sat in disbelief. Some of the attendees came up and embraced the coaches. The questions flowed, but the coach only answered a few of them.

Finally, Jeanie Erickson, Hoss's mother, announced, through her sniffles, "Bill and Lynette are going to need our help. I will call Pastor Johansen tomorrow morning to get a prayer chain going, and we'll get the church's Ladies Aid Auxiliary to put together a meal delivery calendar."

Another parent spoke up, "We live right next to the Natvigs. We've been doing the feeding for them this week. I will get a hold of Bill and let him know that I'll get some of our neighbors to help with his farm and chores. We got the farm covered, Coach."

Other parents floated out ideas for supporting the Natvigs. Coach Kilmer thanked the group for coming and reminded the wrestlers there would be practice the next day. That is when little Wes Sorenson gradually raised his hand. Coach called out, "Yeah, Wes. You want to say something?"

The room went awkwardly silent as people wondered what Wes would possibly have to say. Wes stood up, "Just wondering something. Now... if the basketball team wins the state championship, every player on the roster, even the guys on the bench, gets to say they are state champs. They put it on their letterman's jacket, right?"

Tom Kilmer, not sure of the intent of Wes's

little speech, "I guess that's right."

Wes continued, "I know I am not very good... yet. I know I am "O" and three on varsity and been pinned three times." A few chuckles arose around the room. "But I've been thinking. If we won the state championship as a team, I would get to put "State Champ" on my letterman's jacket even if I never win a match."

"Fair enough," the coach smiled at the thought of Wes having "State Champ" on his back and nodded his head. Without warning, Charlie hopped up. "I get it!"

Charlie thought if he understood it, everyone else must have already got it. But as he scanned around, he met many puzzled faces staring back. "We all know Bingo's goal is to be a state champion. What Wes is saying is if we can win the state title as a team. Bingo will be a state champion. Man, that is cool," Charlie noted while giving Wes a double thumbs up.

Wes continued shaking his head yes as Charlie beamed with pride for following Wes's reasoning. Charlie went on, "We all have to do our share and get to the state tournament. My best shot at it will be at 155-pounds. Sorry, Mark, but I'm coming down."

"I'm okay with that. I've been thinking about cutting to 45 anyway," Mark replied.

Pete chirped in, "I haven't been cutting weight at all, so I make sixty-seven by next week."

147

Spider volunteered, "I've been making 105 pretty easily, I think I can make it to 98, and Kevin can follow me down to 105." He glanced at Kevin across the room. Kevin responded with a smile and an 'all in' nod.

The buzz continued around the room. Coach held up his open hand like a stop sign to redirect individuals' attention. When he felt the group's attention back on him, he continued, "Alright, alright,...winning a title is a lofty goal, and we haven't discussed it much as a team. But I believe we can do it. We are a pretty solid team right now, but I think you are right. If we get a little leaner, we will fill in our holes. Some of you are already at your optimum weight, while others can trim body fat percentage and still be strong. We'll examine each of you individually and set up a plan."

A voice in the back of the room perked up, "You will have a hole at 185-pounds." All eyes turned to see Drew Parker standing up. "I'm going to go to eighty-five for Bing."

Coach Kilmer, "Sorry, Drew, we all know what you need to do, and we all want you to succeed at Nebraska. We are proud of you, and the Cornhuskers coaches have a vision and plan for your future. As much as we would need you in the lineup, I cannot let you do it. We'll talk about it later."

"Don't need to talk later, and I don't know how you can stop me, Coach. I'll be in the lineup at 185 in three weeks, versus Waverly."

CHAPTER 13
DETERMINATION

A few minutes before seven o'clock in the morning, three Spartans, in their sweatpants and hooded sweatshirts pulled up over their heads, tried to stay warm by dancing around the gas pumps at the Texaco Gas Station at the end of the Main Street business district. The iconic station's drive-through gas pump area underneath the building's second story provided an automobile entrance to the gas pumps from either Main Street or 3rd Avenue.

A Firestone Tires neon light hung in the second-story grease-covered window above the pumps. Atop the window, a pole extended out over the main street sidewalk. A circular, porcelain sign with a green "T" inside a red star hung from the pole. Covering the office's drive-through wall was a vast, colorful twelve-foot by twenty-foot United States road map. Next to the giant map, looking out the office window, stood a life-size cardboard cut-out of a man in a green uniform and a green

149

policeman-type hat greeting customers. The cardboard man held a sign reading, "You Can Trust Your Car to The Man Who Wears the Star!" The Legion Club sat on the corner across Main Street with a church on each of the other corners.

For the first day of school after Christmas break, the team decided to do something special to demonstrate to the town and the school their support of Bing Natvig and how much he meant to them. Drew and Pete, stride for stride, passed in front of the large red brick Methodist Church and cut diagonally across the intersection. They joined the small group by the gas pumps, but in a matter of minutes, wrestlers came jogging in from all directions, gathering under the gas station's covered area. Charlie led a band of nineteen farm kids who drove into town, parked at the high school, and ran collectively to join the gathering.

A cloud rose from the breath of more than thirty kids, dressed in grey sweatpants and various colored hooded sweatshirts as they were bouncing up and down to keep warm, waiting under the cover of the station. Charlie checked the office clock by putting his hands on the side of his eyes to prevent the glare as he leaned against the window and announced, "It's time. Let's go!"

Someone hollered out, "Here comes Coach," as Coach Kilmer picked up his pace to merge with the teenagers. Charlie razzed him, "You're late. What? Mrs. Coach keep you a little busy this morning?"

They all laughed and looked at the coach, knowing what Charlie implied. Luckily, the coach's cheeks were already red from the cold, so no one recognized his embarrassment as he acknowledged the comment, "Funny one, Charlie." His retort drew more chuckles.

Charlie joined Drew and Hoss at the front of the group. The wrestlers organized the unity display for Bingo, so Coach gave way to their leadership, melding into the pack next to Spider and Jose.

Hoss shouted out, "1, 2, 3!" The gang answered back, "Spartans!"

The hearty mixture headed onto Main Street, taking over the southbound half of the street as they jogged collectively past the Court House. The streetlights were still on, but the sky was brightening on the eastern horizon. At the end of the three blocks of the business district, they crossed the railroad tracks onto the half-block of red brick street pavers next to Beadle Park.

Coach Kilmer lost his focus as he searched the tree-covered park for a familiar exhibit. In their attempt to learn more about Cresco, the coach and his wife probably knew more history of the community than most local citizens. How a small town in the middle of the country, far from any ocean, produced five United States Navy Admirals fascinated Coach Kilmer. Furthermore, the large World War I German Naval magnetic mine hanging

151

from a heavy-duty metal frame in the heart of Beadle Park intrigued him incredibly. No one offered him a valid reason why a town in Iowa displayed a German war artifact in their park. He recalled sitting at the Natvig kitchen table and having a hilarious dialog with Bingo and his parents over the mine. They decided German soldiers slipped into Cresco and planted the mine in Beadle Park in case one of the Cresco's admirals brought a destroyer home with him.

Coach nearly came to a complete stop staring at the silver-painted, three-foot round mine, recalling the laughter of that morning with Bingo. His mind drifted to going fishing with him and their heart-to-heart talks.

"Hey, Coach! You okay?"

He turned and hurried to re-join the gang where Main Street crossed Highway 9, at the only stoplight in Cresco. A school bus driver stopped at the lights, allowing the joggers to circle inside the intersection in front of it. The driver honked and let her young riders slide down the windows and holler words of encouragement to the troop.

Charlie led the stampede back up the slight slope of the brick street towards the business district again. A silver corrugated metal grain elevator stood opposite the park on the east side of the brick road. As the boys ran through the shadow of the eight-story structure, the granary staff who had assembled outside the office door, clapped.

Even though gloves and mittens muffled the sound, the kids appreciated it and acknowledged the applause with waves as they jogged by the elevator.

More vehicles appeared on Main Street, and the drivers honked and waved at the group, not entirely understanding the whole meaning of the team's early morning run. A few store owners came out of their doors to acknowledge the squad as they trekked by on the other half of Main Street. A quartet of men having their morning coffee in the Main Street Diner stepped outside and expressed their support for Spartan wrestling by raising their cups in a toast.

Cutting through the Texaco Station, as snowflakes floated down, they ran the remaining blocks down the little hill and up the other side, arriving at the high school fifteen minutes before school began. Parents dropping their students off for school hailed the wrestling team with a thunder of horn honking. The police chief pulled the squad car up on the sidewalk in front of the main building. To the wrestlers' surprise, he turned his lights and siren on as they came onto the school campus.

Elementary and junior high students gathered around the three-story high school's front entrance and carried on the cheering as two students held the doors open for the squad. The pack continued by jogging up the stairs to the main floor, down the hall past the office and trophy case, and towards the gymnasium. Students and staff members clapped and cheered as the wrestlers moved to their final destination. The school cheerleaders met the grapplers inside the gym entrance and sang out, "B-I-N-G-O, B-I-N-G-O, and Bingo was his name-O!" The collection circled the gym, returned to the ensemble of girls, gave them high fives, and thanked them for being there.

"Bring it in!" The assemblage, with the cheerleaders, packed around Hoss. Each of them extended a high hand towards the middle of the group. "Bingo on three... 1, 2, 3!"

"BINGO!" It echoed down the hallway as the guys headed to the steep concrete steps to the locker room to shower and dress to arrive to class on time. The coach could not have been prouder.

With the help of Lori Kilmer, Drew began his diet and extended exercise plan. She planned his meals and set weight loss goals with him. Determined, Drew concentrated on losing eighteen pounds in three weeks, and having Mrs. Coach as his trainer made it possible to hit or exceed his daily goals without jeopardizing his health or strength. His mother made his meals and snacks, and Lori monitored his body fat percentage using a skinfold caliper. Already a fit athlete, he initiated his weight loss at ten percent body fat.

He lost nine pounds in the first week without limiting his water intake. Hitting a mental wall in the middle of the second week, it became harder to climb out of bed to do his additional morning run. It seemed the smell of food was everywhere, and everyone had a snack to tempt him. With Coach's permission, he avoided the cafeteria during his lunch break and snuck into the wrestling room with his lunch in the paper bag his mother had packed. He savored every little bite of orange, the carrot slices, and a few celery sticks with peanut butter. Having eaten his simple meal, Drew folded up his paper bag and put it in his back pocket to take home and reuse again the next day. Some of his teammates who were also cutting weight showed up in the wrestling room to keep him company. They all had a rumble in their stomachs from skipping meals, except for Hoss, who rolled in for comradery.

By the beginning of the third week, Drew's body fat ratio read less than seven percent, but his attitude received a boost when he tipped the scale below a hundred and ninety pounds. Charlie understood the loneliness of hammering out the last few pounds, so he joined Drew during PE class, running the gymnasium's perimeter while the rest of the class played games. With his sweats on and hood pulled up tight over his head, Drew appreciated his friend jogging at his shoulder. He would still fast and limit his fluids the last day and a half to make the weight class.

Lori Kilmer tried to engage the rest of the crew by discussing dieting with them. They listened to her and tweaked their meals somewhat by adding more fruits and vegetables. For the most part, they

155

did not possess the self-discipline of Drew, so they tackled their weight loss by skipping meals and doing extra running in rubber suits. Spider and Kent established their scratch weight for the first dual in the new year, delegating a content Wes to the junior varsity lineup. Charlie and the rest of the guys moved down a weight class for the next dual meet. Without Bing and Drew in the lineup, the squad, now under Hoss and Charlie's leadership, came together, delivering four more dual meet victories to begin the new year.

The varsity team attended another tournament in Caledonia, Minnesota, held the third weekend in January. Minnesota wrestling powerhouses, including Albert Lea High School, Fridley High School, and the host school, packed the eight team tournament. Coach wanted his wrestlers to experience another tough tournament but knew they needed a break from cutting weight, so he entered each of them up a weight class. Spider took second, Jose lost in the finals, Charlie eked out a gold medal at 167, and the ref raised Hoss's hand in the heavyweight division finals. A pair of third-place medals and two fourth places helped the squad to a solid second-place finish for the Spartans as the wrestlers experienced some intense matches.

Wes, back in the varsity lineup at 98-pounds for this tournament, won a consolation match for his first varsity victory and his teammates exploded on him in jubilation at the edge of the mat.

CHAPTER 14
CHARLIE

The returning conference dual meet champions, with three returning state qualifiers, expected to defend their title. The Waverly Go-Hawks presented a solid lineup with a team dual meet record equal to the Spartans- seven wins and only one loss. On paper, even if Bingo competed, Waverly would have been favored to win the dual meet. Brad Lentz, who finished third in the state tournament last season at 119-pounds, led the Waverly grapplers. Now at 126-pounds, Lentz ranked first in the state and was slated to wrestle Jose.

An hour before the junior varsity meet, both squads were in weight lines from lightest to heaviest in the Waverly Boys locker room on each side of a bench running down the aisle between banks of metal lockers. The referee stood at the front of the lines behind the standing medical beam scale, ensuring it was calibrated and balanced out at zero. Both school's coaches held pens and clipboards as they stood on each side of the scale next to the referee, ready to record each of their wrestlers' actual weight, one weight class at a time, beginning with the 98 pounders. The coaches watched the referee make a final adjustment to the scale to ensure it balanced out correctly.

Standing with nothing on but their underwear, neither team's wrestlers made eye contact with their rivals in the opposing line. They attempted to check out each other's muscular frames without being accused of eying another guy's body. The less-developed kids were embarrassed by their lack of muscle tone or lack of body hair or both. Secretly, each of them in the room was jealous of Drew's chiseled body and six-pack abs.

Except for the heavyweights, many athletes had not eaten in the last twenty-four or more hours. At the same time, many of them restricted their liquids for the same amount of time. Some of the athletes spit in a can or plastic bottle all day to shed their last pound.

They were easily irritated, starving, thirsty, and wanted this to be over as soon as possible. No one talked much, other than a few small conversations between teammates. The one exception was Brad Lentz, who had a reputation of intimidating his opponent with a few verbal jabs. Lentz opened up on Jose.

"Hey, Beaner. Do you know who I am?

Undefeated and ranked number one in the state, man. I hear they call you Beaner, because of all the refried beans you eat."

Not new to Jose, who's heard this type of racist verbal attack many times before. He ignored Lentz and kept staring towards the front of the line.

"HEY, BEANER! Can't speak English? I'm talking to you, SPIC... I'm goin' kick your brown..."

Before he said another word, Charlie seized him by the throat with his giant left hand and shoved him up against the locker, stuck his right index finger in his face, and lifted him, so his heels almost came off the ground. It happened so instantaneously that Lentz's eyes glazed over. Rollie instinctively followed Charlie's lead, grabbed Lentz's left wrist, and trapped it against the locker. Seeing Rollie, Pete trapped the other arm. The Waverly squad members did not even have time to react before the whole Spartan crew, except for Jose, crowded around Charlie and Lentz. Hoss strategically put himself between the group and the coaches, shielding the scene from them with his enormous body. The coaches and referee, puzzled by the commotion, were so stunned by the noise they hardly reacted. Drew eyed the Waverly team to see if any of them wished to come to Lentz's rescue. The body language around the Waverly bunch signaled no willingness to step up.

"His name is Jose! Hoe - SAY!!" Dragging out the 'oh' sound in Hoe. "AND I would be careful what

159

the next frickin' word comes out of your mouth. Get it?" Lentz nodded the best he could, hardly able to breathe, let alone move.

"Anybody else have any shit to say?" Charlie glanced around as he slowly released his grip. "Jose is my friend and our teammate, and we'll be glad to settle it right here and now. The hell with the mat."

The Cresco kids checked the Waverly wrestlers to see any of them were stepping up. None did. Both sets of coaches began to push their way through the high schoolers.

"Break it up! Get back in your lines!" But by then, the Spartans started to move back on their own. Charlie let go of Lentz.

Brad Lentz's coach asked him, "What's going on?"

Lentz made eye contact with Charlie, then at Jose, and replied to his coach, "Nuthin', Coach."

Jose kept a stoic face, but on the inside, he glowed. Jose could call his colleagues teammates and friends, and he felt they believed in him for the first time, and he could now count on them. Coach Kilmer eyed Drew. Drew shrugged his shoulders and shook his head no as if to say not to worry.

No one else uttered a sound during the weigh-ins as they returned to the standard procedure. Alternating between teams and starting with the lightest weight class, wrestlers would step on the scale followed by immediately pouring fluids back into their bodies the moment they stepped off.

Throwing their clothes back on, they would wait for their friends so they could go to the gym and chow down the food they had packed along.

Spider made 98 by a quarter of a pound. Drew slipped out of his underwear and exhaled loudly when he stepped onto the scale. "One hundred eighty-five pounds exactly," the referee announced. A broad grin grew on Drew's face, and a slight smile crept across Coach Kilmer's face as he gave Drew a wink. Shouts of "Yeah!" "Great job!" "Way to go, Drew!" erupted from his friends. Drew and Hoss slapped high-fives as they exchanged places.

They were 'all in' for Bing, but tonight the adrenalin escalated to a new high. Spider started the meet with the first match, competing against a junior with only two losses on the season. Spider gave up an early takedown and an escape to fall behind three to zero in the second period. Before the second period ended, Spider hit a high crotch, threw his leg into a cross-body ride, hit a mean cross face grabbing the far arm, and "turked" his opponent to his back, and holding him there the rest of the period. Spider hit a switch in the third period and then overpowered the junior with a nearside cradle for the pin.

The Spartans won two of the next three matches before Jose took the mat. Brad Lentz warmed up behind his teammates, ready to go. His coach made a calculated judgment to send his talented 127-pound junior varsity wrestler out to take on Jose and move Lentz up a weight. A classy decision and Coach Kilmer understood and appreciated it. The Waverly coach would not let whatever happened in the locker room escalate to the dual meet. Strategically, the opposing coach thought he could collect two victories with his junior varsity wrestler beating Jose and Lentz pinning Rollie. But Jose made short work of his unexpected foe by using a double cowcatcher to counter the Waverly wrestler's fireman's carry takedown attempt. Jose threw him to his back and stepped on top, hooked both foe's legs with his own legs. Dubbed a 'Saturday Night Special' ride, the Waverly grappler was pinned before thirty seconds rolled off the clock. Jose's buddies leaped out of their chairs, responding to the referee slapping the mat, and rushed to the edge of the mat to greet Jose as soon as the referee raised his hand.

Lentz pinning Bingo's replacement was an easy assumption for the entire Waverly fan base and coaching staff, but Rollie wrestled a heck of a match, losing 5-2. Waverly won the next two matches to cut Cresco's lead to 21-12.

Charlie's intensity from the locker room continued. Wrestling a returning state qualifier, Charlie took him down in the first period and turned him with a wrist lock and a half-nelson for two back points. In the second period, he reversed him and turned him again for a three-point near fall. With

Charlie leading 9-0 opening the third period, the Waverly kid chose down and attempted a stand-up. Charlie locked his hands tightly around his opponent's hips from behind him, picked him up in the air, and drove him sideways down on his shoulder and head with a "bam," nearly knocking him out. A significant "ouch" soared from the stands. The referee stopped the match and disqualified Charlie.

A few boos rang out from the Cresco fans, but neither Coach Kilmer nor Charlie put up an argument. Charlie shook the kid's hand as protocol demanded but did not apologize. He walked off, and his teammates met him as he came off the mat in silent respect. No one wanted to see a wrestler get hurt, even a rival, but they were all okay with giving up the six team points instead of scoring a Spartan win. Still making a statement, Charlie intentionally sought out Jose and gave him a high five.

Cresco won two of the last three matches as Drew used a driving double leg for a takedown. He then climbed up on top, slipped in an armbar, and locked up the opposite wrist. As he walked around his adversary's head, he cranked his opponent over to his back for the fall. Finishing the dual meet, Hoss stepped on the mat next and hit a quick lateral drop to record a pin within the first minute.

The local sports headline read, "Wow, Cresco 33 Waverly 21", with the first line reading, "It was worse than the score indicated."

163

CHAPTER 15

SECTIONALS

Lori immediately greeted her husband as he skipped into the back porch. She grasped a glass of red wine and was in the mood to celebrate. Riding along with Karla Parker, Lori had spent the day at the Sectional Tournament kicking off the early morning with her cooler and two decks of cards. She remembered last year's Sectional Tournament so vividly when only Bing Natvig advanced and how depression set in for her husband and the team in the wake of Joel Parker's accident.

What a difference a year makes. Tom hoped to qualify six wrestlers to Districts, but nine wrestlers advanced plus one alternate with a phenomenal group effort that day. Tom gave his spouse a wonderful hug, and they kissed each other. She asked him if he wanted some wine, but he declined and snatched a can of beer from the refrigerator as they passed through the kitchen to the living room. He did not drink often, but tonight a beer sounded terrific as a celebration.

He popped the top of his Schell's Original 'Deer Brand' and plopped down on the couch next to Lori. They sat hip-to-hip in front of the shut-off television and talked about every kid and every match. "Kevin came out of nowhere to upset the number one seed from Decorah in the semi-finals and then beat the Waukon kid in the finals, incredible!" Tom boasted, "We only lost two matches today I thought we should have won. Spider made a mistake and got caught in a cradle and got pinned in the finals. He bounced back by winning his wrestle-back match. Man, he was in control the whole time. I wasn't too worried, but those winner-goes-on and the loser-goes-home matches can be gut-wrenching. He is such a great kid and hates to lose. Jose's a puzzle in the finals. Like he didn't want to win it at the end. Oh well, he's moving on."

Tom went on and on, telling Lori every detail of each match as if Lori had not been there. Though she witnessed every match, she loved the excitement her husband expressed as he talked about each teen, and she let him jabber. Spider, Jose, Rollie, Pete, and Mark finished second while Cresco crowned four champions with Kevin, Charlie, Drew, and Hoss. The Spartans stormed away with the team title.

An hour later, they stopped talking about wrestling and proceeded towards a bit of romance.

The couple loved each other completely. Tom put his arm around Lori and kissed her on her nose. Cheerfully, she giggled a little and tickled his ribs. The busy wrestling season with weekends and late nights did not leave time for romance, then the doorbell rang, interrupting the amorousness.

The pair, baffled by the noise, spoke out, "Who could that be? It's 12:30 at night?"

The bell rang again and again as Tom sprang up and darted to the front entrance. He turned the porch light on, opened the main door, and recognized a bloody Spider standing outside the glass storm door. Spider's left eye was nearly swollen closed, and tears were coming down his cheek.

"LORI! Come help me!" as he opened the storm door. "Get in here, Spider! What happened?"

Tom grabbed him under his arm, helping him up the step and through the front door. Tom saw blood dripping from Spider's lip and noticed his other eye appearing bruised but not nearly as bad as his left. Spider held his right wrist as he came into the Kilmer's living room.

"Oh, my God!" Lori cried, "were you in a car accident? Is anyone else hurt?"

"My...my dad," Spider sniveled as blood bubbled out his nose. "He was waiting for me when I got ho... home." Holding back his tears. "I wasn't... I didn't think he would be there."

Lori helped Spider remove his winter coat

167

and together, the couple laid him down on the couch. Lori put a pillow under his head and another pillow under his knees.

"He doesn't like it when I lose. He heard down at the Legion I got pinned... he gets mad when I lose but... getting pinned.... he was so pissed. He yelled at me,... called me a pussy. Mom hollered at him to stop and...and he, a... he slapped her." Spider sniffled and took a deep breath. "He slapped her so hard...she fell, and I grabbed him, and...um, I didn't fight back. I never fight back. I never fight back."

"Tom, get me a wet washcloth," Lori politely insisted.

Tom headed to the bathroom, stared back at Spider, and paused as he remembered how Joe always mentioned how odd it was to see Spider coming into practices all bruised up the day following matches. Tom continued into the bathroom but was thinking back to Joe's comments, and it dawned on him that Spider arrived at school only battered on the days after matches he lost. Guilt set in as Tom wished he would have paid closer attention to Joe's observations and perception. Running cold water over two washcloths, he squeezed them out and brought them to Lori. He looked down again at Spider and then went to the kitchen.

Lori hollered for her husband to bring her some ice, but he did not answer. She called out again and then heard the Nova rev up as it pulled out of the garage. The sound diminished as the car sped away down the alleyway.

"Spider, you're going to be alright. I'm going to take care of you."

She put one cold, wet washcloth over his eyes and the other on his lip. Lori scampered to the kitchen to get a warm cloth. Retrieving an ice cube tray out of the freezer, she twisted it to pop the cubes out on a towel and folded the towel over. The towel would have to do until she found the ice bags. Returning to Spider, Lori put the ice towel on his eyes and began to dab his face with the warm cloth washing the blood away. Once she cleaned Spider up, Lori found a pair of ice bags in a storage box on the porch. She loaded ice from the freezer into the bags, replaced the towel on his eyes with one of them, and put the other bag on his wrist.

Twenty minutes later, Spider fell asleep. Lori gave him a little kiss on the forehead and took the ice bags to the freezer to refreeze the partially melted cubes. Getting a blanket down from the shelf in the front coat closet, she untied Spider's shoes, removed them, and set them aside. Lori covered him up, tucked the blanket around his sides, and wrapped his feet. Spider stirred a bit and, without opening his eyes, said, "Thank you."

She pulled her wing-backed armchair over next to the couch. Getting down on her knees in front of Spider, Lori began drawing his face like her mother drew hers when she was a child. She gently

169

massaged him using a single finger, first circling his face, then circled each facial feature as if drawing them on. Being careful not to irritate his wounds, she continued to caress his face until she recognized his heavy breathing and deep sleep. Lori crawled up off her knees and sat back in her chair. She put her hand on the top of his head as he slept. She sweetly whispered, "It's alright. You'll be okay, Spider."

Lori closed her eyes and, in a few minutes, fell asleep herself. The sound of the back door opening woke her up. Tom quietly slid immediately into the bathroom. Hearing him turn on the water in the sink, she sounded, "Tom?"

"Yeah, Hun. Just washing my hands."

He came out of the bathroom, drying his hands with a towel. Setting the towel on the dining room table, he came into the living room and knelt on the floor in front of Spider and Lori. He studied Spider resting peacefully on the couch as Lori kept massaging his head. "Is he okay?"

"I think so," she whispered back.

Tom rested his arm and head on Lori's lap. Looking at Spider, Tom reached over Spider's chest with his other arm and gently cuddled him. Lori lovingly placed her free hand on her husband's head. She noticed Tom's knuckles were red with scratches but let it go. They all fell asleep.

CHAPTER 16
DISTRICTS

A competitor needed to finish in the top two at districts to advance to the state tournament. Coach kept Spider out of contact wrestling during the week to give him time to mend. With a massive black eye and taped-up wrist, the freshman wrestled with tenacity, astounding his coaches, teammates, and fans. Spider swept the 98-pound bracket in complete control, avenging his loss the week earlier in the sectional tournament and not giving up a single point in three matches.

Subsequently to his unexpected sectional tournament championship, Kevin surprised the Cresco fan base by placing second, qualifying for the state meet. Jose finished second again after he coasted to the finals, before losing 1-0. Rollie hurt his knee in his final match of the day but hung on to win the match to qualify for the state tournament. Pete settled for being an alternate to state, allowing him to travel with the team to the state tournament and weigh-in. If one of the qualifiers, for some reason, is unable to participate or does not make weight, he would replace them. It does not happen often, but Pete would practice and keep his weight down to be ready if it does. Both Charlie and Hoss lost in the finals and took home runners-up medallions. Drew destroyed his competition, winning the district title 8-3.

Before the Cresco fans celebrated the District Team Championship, Hoss brought his teammates to an isolated hallway on the backside of the gymnasium. For the most part, they were in a cheerful mood piling on each other as they jostled to find a place to sit. Depressed from suffering a heart-wrenching defeat, Pete got into the playfulness as his disappointment in not qualifying for the state meet began to diminish in the light of the team's success. Hoss stood up in front of his buddies without the coaches there. "Uff Da!" he shouted out, expressing a little of his Scandinavian heritage, and pounded his chest. "Man! We did it!"

"But…" Hoss's tone mellowed, "don't forget, winning districts wasn't our goal. It's a big deal, but we have a bigger fish to fry."

Charlie chipped in, "Kilmer would like to hear that!"

Hoss smirked in response to Charlie and continued the seriousness of his talk. "We are going to show everyone we are a team on a mission, and Pete, you are going to lead us to the podium."

Unaware of the impromptu team meeting, the coaches remained in the gym, talking with parents as they waited for the trophy presentation. When the loudspeaker announced the Cresco Spartans as the District Champions, Coach Kilmer and Coach Hall turned to see their wrestlers in a line, shoulder-to-shoulder, at the far end of the gym. Pete stepped out from the middle of the group. The remaining wrestlers locked hands and raised them in the air. With Pete in front, the line of Spartans walked side-by-side the length of the gym floor to the tiered podium.

Coach Hall started to move out of the bleachers to join the team but felt Tom grab his arm. "Hey, they have a plan. Let's see it play out...Give 'em the spotlight."

Pete remained down front as his teammates climbed onto the three levels of the platform. Pete accepted the team trophy, held it above his head, and turned around to face his teammates. He shouted, "Get it?" and the gang answered back, "GOT IT!"

"Holy cow, Tom. How about that. They're going to do it, aren't they?"

Shaking his head up and down in amazement, Tom replied, "Yes, yes they are."

With the growing number of schools with wrestling programs and the increased fan enthusiasm throughout Iowa, the Iowa High School State Wrestling Tournament moved from northeast

173

Iowa to a larger venue and more central location with Des Moines Veterans Memorial Auditorium.

Walking into the auditorium resembled walking into a vast empty barn. It didn't take long for Veterans Memorial Auditorium to be dubbed 'The Barn' by the Iowa fans, kids, and sportswriters. The nickname resulted not only for its emptiness but also for its outside appearance of an oversized barn. It is an appropriate nickname, considering most participants and fans were coming from the farm or farming communities.

The trip to Des Moines would be the first time Spider, Kevin, Jose, and Pete walked into such a large arena, and it would be the first time Spider, Kevin, and Jose ever stayed in a hotel. None of them ever wrestled in such a building and in front of a crowd nearly ten times larger than the district tournament. Charlie, Hoss, and Rollie visited 'The Barn' last year, viewing the tournament from the stands to support Bingo. Drew experienced the auditorium's vastness compared to the Cresco gym as an alternate his sophomore year.

Even though Tom experienced the Minnesota State Tournament as an assistant coach, Minneapolis's arena and crowd size did not compare to the Iowa tournament. He remembered being intimidated last year walking in the doors of 'The Barn' with Bingo. Luckily, his assistant coach kept him grounded. Tom appreciated Joe as a fantastic motivator, so he delegated the boys'

174

mental preparation to his seasoned assistant. He knew they were in good hands.

On Tuesday, the day before the band of grapplers headed to Des Moines, Coach Hall met the guys as they came into the locker room when school was over. "Check your weight and then put your street clothes back on. We're going on a road trip."

Joe sat behind the wheel of the fifteen-passenger school van parked behind the gymnasium when the high schoolers came out the back door of the locker room. They repeatedly asked where there were going as Coach Kilmer slid into the shotgun seat, but neither coach responded.

The trip began with a stop at a small dairy four miles west of town. The sun reflected sharply on the drifts of snow up against the barn and highlighted the tops of a picket fence sticking up out of the snow that defined the yard. In front of the two-story whitewashed house, which desperately needed a new paint job, stood an arching trellis greeting visitors at the front of the shoveled sidewalk leading to the front porch. Joe Hall guided the van around the house to the open area cleared of snow in front of the weathered, red-painted barn. Two ten-gallon stainless steel milk cans sat on the concrete loading dock connected to the barn.

"What are we doing at a dairy?" Charlie piped up, lowering his eyebrows, scowling, and then looked towards Jose. "Jose and I got enough work to do when we get home tonight."

175

"Do you know who's farm this is?" Joe asked. When no one spoke, he continued, "Well, hop out, and let's go find out."

As the gang climbed out of the van, a sixty-year-old farmer in his blue striped overalls with a long-sleeved cotton collar shirt and rubber barn boots appeared on the loading dock door. "Hey, guys! Come on in." He surprised them by calling each of them by name. He shook their hands and introduced himself as Ron as they came through the lean-to door and entered the milking parlor.

Not as modern as the Spiegler dairy, but exceptionally clean, the dairy hinted the 'not so sweet' smell of souring milk. The parallel milking parlor had three metal-framed stalls lined up on each side of an eight-foot-wide interior concrete walkway. The elevated stalls were three feet higher than the walkway, so the cows' udders were at hand level when milking. Ron penned one of his Holstein cows in a stall.

The warm, almost hot temperature in the milking parlor forced the guys to peel off their hats and coats as they gathered around Ron and Joe in the middle of the walkway farmer's called the 'pit.'

Uncomfortable with the thought of speaking in front of a group, Ron initially declined the coach's request, but Joe's persistence prevailed. A reluctant Ron finally agreed, flattered that Joe thought he had something important to offer to the gang. Joe spoke, "I know you guys have seen Ron at our wrestling meets. And I can tell you, he doesn't miss many of them. He wants to talk to you before you go off to the state tournament."

Rollie said, "We know Ron. He goes to church with me, Mark, and Kent."

Joe went on, "Then you know his last name is Peckham. Tom Peckham is his son." The guys glanced at each other embarrassed they did not know who Ron was, but at the same time, they were in awe in the presence of wrestling royalty. "Tom's a three-time state champion. He went on to wrestle at Iowa State University and was a two-time national champion and, in 1968, made the USA Olympic Team and finish fourth at the Mexico City Olympics."

These guys needed no introduction to Tom Peckham. Everybody in Cresco knew his name and accomplishments. Ron launched his story, "Joe here wanted me to show you where Tom grew up. My dad built our home in 1905. It seemed more like a three-room cabin when I grew up in the twenties and thirties. We didn't have electricity in the house until 1950. We used a hand pump in the kitchen for drinking and cooking water but no bathroom. There was an outhouse until we remodeled the house after the war. I guess Tom grew up right here in this barn. You don't know it, but Coach Joe was his junior high coach and got him going with rasslin'. Then Joe was Chris Flanagan's assistant when Tom was in high school." The boys peered at Coach Hall. Joe tried not

177

to smile but could not help himself, proud to have helped coach such a talented wrestler.

"Charlie and Jose know all 'bout milking. They got at least three times as many milking cows as I do. It's gall darn hard work. Isn't it, boys?" Charlie and Jose were shaking their heads in agreement. "But it used to be a lot harder. When Tom was in grade school, we milked the cows by hand. Squeezing cow teats for a couple of our hours in the morning and again at night sure makes your grip strong." Ron put his hands out front to demonstrate milking a cow, squeezing his fists as he moved them up and down. The guys laughed amusingly at Ron's hand motions, making him appear as if he was dancing.

"Harold always said he never coached a kid with a stronger grip than our Tom." No one needed to remind the kids "Harold" referred to Harold Nichols, the Iowa State Wrestling Coach who grew up in Cresco.

"So, I wanna see if you guys can get any milk out of old Gertrude here." Ron smiled as he grabbed a stainless-steel bucket and put it under the fenced-in Holstein. He used a 'teat dip' cup and towel to disinfect and clean Gertrude's teats. "Who's first?"

The group expected Charlie to go first and show off, but to everyone's surprise, Jose, the kid who always waits until last, stepped forward. The rest of them huddled around to watch him. Jose gently massaged Gertrude's teats to make her comfortable with him. The guys heard the milk spray hit the bottom of the stainless steel as Jose squeezed and pulled.

Ron declared, "Dang! Way to go, Jose! You're an old pro at this! Who's next?"

Jose did not express any emotion but was proud of himself, knowing he did something the others probably could not do or at least not do as well. He aimed one of Gertrude's teats away from the bucket and sprayed milk on Hoss's leg, startling him. Hoss jumped back, bellowing, "Hey! What are you doing?" Other than Hoss, they all broke up as Jose smiled.

One at a time, each boy, along with both coaches, attempted to milk the cow. Most of them produced limited success. Charlie remained unusually quiet. It took a bit of time, but he vindicated himself in front of his peers once he got going. "AND that's how it's done, boys!"

Ron continued, "When you got done with a cow, you poured the bucket of milk into the ten-gallon can. My boys hauled the cans to the deck and later lifted them onto the flatbed, and we would take them to the creamery in town and unload them. I can't tell you how many cans Tom picked up and carried around this farm. Jeez, somewhere around the time he went to junior high, we changed over to this parlor with surge milkers. Nice having the pit, so you didn't have to bend over all day, but the boys still poured the surge cans of milk into the

179

ten-gallon cans and moved them. When Tom headed off to college, we added the piping system where the milk gets pumped directly to the holding tank and separator. Not quite as big as your system, Charlie."

"We don't use the milk cans anymore, but if you haven't ever picked one up, try it. I put water in the two cans out on the deck for you." Ron grinned, knowing how heavy ten-gallon cans can be, weighing nearly eighty-five pounds each when full of milk.

"Tom always talked 'bout how he went to state and rassled those city boys. He said they were scared to death havin' to rassle a farm boy from Cresco. Taking down those city kids was nothin' compared to rassling a Holstein into a shoot," Ron beamed. "You see?...Those city kids will be scared of you. So, you guys go down to Des Moines and kick some butt."

The boys were excited to know more and asked lots of questions. "What was it like to wrestle at Iowa State? The nationals? At the Olympics? Did you go watch? Where is Tom now? What is he doing?" Ron tried to answer their questions and was pleased they were so interested.

Coach Hall finally interrupted and stated, "It's time to go." Both coaches showed Ron their gratitude as they shooed the boys towards the door. Putting on their coats and hats, they thanked Ron and stepped out on the loading dock. Each one stopped and tried to lift the ten-gallon milk can up.

Kent let out, "Frick'n shit," as he tried to lift one of the cans. He lifted the can in the air a foot and a half using both hands, almost dropping it as he put it back down.

Hoss pushed Kent out of the way. "Here, let a man show you how to do this." He grasped a ten-gallon can handle in each hand and, with a grunt, picked each one up. "There ya go." He put them down almost as fast as he picked them up.

Charlie mocked, "Come on, MAN, pack them over here." Cracking the group up.

"Let's go," Joe said. "I got a little surprise for you guys."

"Cooler than hanging out with Tom Peckham's dad?" Hoss honestly inquired.

"Bingo came home this afternoon."

"Seriously?"

"His dad called us last night, said they would be home after lunch today, and Bing wanted to see you guys before you left."

"What are we waiting for? Let's get going," Rollie shouted out. They all scrambled to the van.

Bing's father stood on the back porch, greeting the kids as they arrived at the Natvig farm. He called each by name and gave them a handshake and a pat on the back as he stood in the doorway leading into the porch. "Go on into the kitchen. Lynette is waiting for you."

The boys came bounding into the kitchen,

181

and other than Jose, each took turns hugging Bing's mother. Jose, not knowing the Natvigs, held back. Lynette turned to him, "Come here, Jose." She grabbed him, wrapped her arms around him, and kissed him on the cheek.

"Thanks for coming." She turned to the group. "Bing has been waiting for you. He will be so happy to see you. He's wearing a mask over his mouth and nose to protect him from germs that may make him sick. As much as you might want to shake his hand or hug him, we need you to stay away and not touch him. Can you do that?" The boys all agreed and headed into the living room. "I have some fresh chocolate chip cookies if your weight is okay."

They all thanked Lynette and skipped the cookie offer except for Hoss, who snatched up four cookies. He promptly shoveled a whole one into his mouth as he chased his peers into the living room.

The coaches had stayed back on the porch chatting with Bill allowing the cluster to move into the house to see their buddy. They trailed Bill into the kitchen, and Lynette met them with hugs. "Hey, it's so nice to see you, boys." She managed a weak smile.

Bill, Joe, and Tom sat down at their familiar places at the kitchen's family table. Lynette moved the cookies and coffee cups tray to the table and brought a fresh pot of coffee over as she sat down with them.

They overheard the laughter going on in the living room. Charlie's voice stood out, "What happened to your eyebrows?"

Hoss answered, "ah, shut up, Charlie."

"No, seriously, jeez, why did they shave your eyebrows off?"

Coach Hall almost spit his coffee out on the table as Lynette smiled. She had not done a lot of smiling lately.

"Leave it to Charlie." Bill grinned and shook his head.

Bill turned to the coaches, "The chemo hasn't been fun. Besides losing his hair, he throws up four or five times during the couple of days after each treatment. He's got blisters on his tongue, making it hard to eat, and he has lost another five pounds in the last week. He is lucky if he weighs a hundred twenty pounds."

The smile left Lynette's face, "They are talking about more intensive chemo and a possible bone marrow transplant if they can find a compatible donor. None of us is a match." She paused, forced a slight smile, and changed the subject, "Anyway, are the boys ready?"

"I think so. Spider should get to the semi-finals, and who knows 'bout Kent. He's just wrestling out of his mind right now. Hoss will have to beat the kid from Waterloo he lost to in the dual if he gets to the semi-finals round, and Charlie will run into a kid who took fourth last year. Drew is on the opposite

183

side of the bracket from the Algona kid, so that's good. Jose, man, Jose...127 is a loaded weight class, but he certainly can place. We will see. I am worried 'bout Rollie's knee, but he says he is okay."

Joe chimed in, "In other good news, Drew signed his official letter of intent to play football at Nebraska last week and sent it back. He signed it in the counselor's office at school with his mom and his football coaches. Even his junior high coaches were there. Holy Toledo, it was pretty awesome. Drew wants to keep it low-key until the state tournament is over. The Times sent a reporter over to take a picture but agreed to wait to publish it later."

Coach Kilmer stood up from the table. "We need to see Bingo before we go. I brought him a little present."

He grabbed the brown paper grocery sack he brought with him. The adult crew took their coffee cups and moved to the living room. They interrupted Charlie and Hoss sharing a story about their double date to a movie over Christmas break. Showing off for the girls, Hoss found a snow and ice-covered empty parking lot and started spinning 'doughnuts' in the snow. When the car high-centered on a snowbank at the edge of the lot, Hoss made the girls help Charlie push the stuck car out of the snow. While Charlie pushed in the middle of the trunk, the reluctant young ladies positioned themselves on opposite back corners of Hoss's

Dodge Dart. Hoss gunned the gas, spun the rear wheels, shot snow and slush up, covering both girls in a wet, snowing mess from top to bottom.

The laughter steadily increased as the story went on, and then Charlie said, "They were not happy campers. I told them they needed to get out of their wet clothes before they caught a cold, and I would be more than happy to help 'em. Then they got really mad. Made us take them home." The group's roar instantly subsided as the grown-ups entered the room.

Both coaches made regular visits to the Natvig farm to visit Bingo when he was home and occasionally helped with morning chores when the Natvigs were in Rochester, so they were not surprised by Bing's frail appearance.

"Hey, fishing buddy! Brought you a present for our fishing trip to the boundary waters this summer." Coach Kilmer handed Bing the paper sack.

Bingo took the grocery sack, quickly opened it up, and pulled out Coach's well-worn fishing hat with fishing flies and lures attached to the band. Bingo held the hat up in the air and tried to act somber, but you could see him grinning even under his mask. "Now, what would I wanna do with the most UN-luckiest fishing hat in the whole world! Snags were all you caught when you wore this hat! The only time you had success was the time you forgot it at home, and you wore one of my John Deere caps."

185

"Hey, hey, hey, don't be so cruel," Tom answered as the gang snickered at him. "Each one of those hooks has a story to tell…"

Before he concluded his anecdote, Charlie injected, "about the big one that got away!" The laughter gushed out again.

Bing slipped the hat on his head. His eyes, barely observable between the brim of the hat and his face mask, lit up. "Awe, Coach, you know I'll wear it with pride when I show you how to catch fish. I can't wait to get out there with you again. Thanks!"

The conversation circled back to the state wrestling tournament until Coach Hall proclaimed, "Gotta go!"

On the way back to the high school, Coach Hall drove down Main Street to show the kids the community support. The boys had their faces glued to the van windows while they stared at all the signs and window-painted messages aimed at them. As the van approached the Howard County Courthouse, Kent yelled out, "There's Brady!"

Holding a yardstick with a sign attached at the top of it was Brady McKane. The young man with Down-Syndrome stood on the corner, used both hands to hold the sign up in the air. Brady had made the sign himself using different colored markers, and it read, "Go Wrestlers!" with a rainbow drawn over the top of the words. Brady was not alone as more than a dozen students and parents surrounded him. The wrestlers fought for a window spot on the courthouse side of the van to see the gathering. Coach Hall slowed down and honked the horn as the group commenced jumping up and down, cheering and waving. The young men peered out the windows and returned their waves. Wielding the sign back and forth, Brady grinned ear to ear.

The highlight of the downtown tour became the marquee extending over the sidewalk at the Cresco Movie Theater. The black letters contrasted the lit up white background that usually displayed the present movie, but instead, they read, "Good Luck at State." The theater manager had the bordering lights of rolling yellow, green, and red turned on, so the boys easily saw their names in the early darkness of February, "Spider, Kent, Jose, Rollie, Charlie, Pete, Drew, Hoss."

Pete knew as an alternate his odds of stepping on a mat for a match were slim to none, but he was still proud to see his name up on the marquee.

CHAPTER 17

STATE

Instead of pennants, the wrestling cheerleaders constructed ten-inch by ten-inch "BINGO" cards out of white cardstock and distributed them to Cresco fans. The card's front side imitated a BINGO card from the game, with the letters B-I-N-G-O across the top of five columns with five squares in each column. Replacing the numbers on a Bingo game card, the seven participants' weight classes were scattered around all the boxes with the center box labeled as a free square, imitating the game card. A blue eight-inch block blue "C" emblazed the back of the card. The cheerleaders encouraged the fans to stand at the end of a Cresco wrestler's winning match, wave the card in the air, and shout out "BINGO" when the referee raises a Spartan's hand in victory.

The wide variety of warm-ups' colors from over a hundred and eighty different high schools with at least one state qualifier dotted the six

189

wrestling mats covering the floor of Veterans Memorial Auditorium. Fans viewed different intensity levels as wrestlers stretched and rolled around the mat while some sparred lightly in preparation for their matches. In his street clothes, Pete hung out with his teammates on the mat. After holding on to the hope of participating until the last qualifier made weight, the coaches delegated him to the role of team manager. On the bright side of the assignment, Pete would have a ringside seat for matches with the charge of the first-aid kit and supplies.

"Wrestlers, clear the mats!" The announcer bellowed through the loudspeaker, stimulating the adrenaline of every participant and coach in 'The Barn.' The colors flowed off the mats and blended into the stands. Round one was ready to commence.

Striking immediately for the Spartans, Spider set the tone for the first round. Escaping during the second period, he took his opponent down with a body lock throw to his back for a pin. When his hand raised above his head, a loud "BINGO!" led by the cheerleaders, rang out from the stands. Kent used three takedowns and an escape for a 7-2 victory. Another raucous round of "BINGO" sounded as his hand rose in the air.

By the time Jose stepped on the mat, the story of Bingo has spread around the auditorium. Often in post-tournament competitions, fans of schools from the same conference tend to root for each other when competing against schools from other areas of the state. The camaraderie between the fans of the northeast Iowa schools became noticeably apparent as different cheerleaders approached the Cresco cheer squad and asked for BINGO cards. When Jose's hand ascended in victory following a 6-3 decision, the shout of "BINGO" more than doubled as blue and white Bingo cards waved throughout the arena.

Rollie tried to wrestle on his taped-up injured knee but ended up forfeiting his match after falling behind 5-0 going into the third period. Rollie's loss did not slow down the Spartan freight train, however. Charlie prevailed 6-2, Drew pinned his challenger in the second period, and Hoss finished the round with the quickest fall of the day with his seventeen-second pin using a sagging head and arm throw. The "BINGO" shouts kept coming!

With his first-round loss, Rollie became the only Cresco wrestler to have another match on day one. Rollie, in obvious pain, limped out on the mat for his consolation match against an over-confident veteran from Marion. The Marion contestant took a weak single-leg shot off the whistle to Rollie's right leg. Rollie sprawled, snapped him down, and spun to the side. With a tight waist and arm chop, Rollie broke him down to his stomach. He kept the pressure on the back of his head, holding his adversary flat on the mat as he worked for a far wrist lock. When he tied up the wrist, he rolled it under

191

and ran a near-side half-nelson, sweeping the kid to his back. Rollie sunk the half-nelson in deeper, slid down chest-to-chest, and heard the slap of the mat.

Day one of the state tournament could not have gone much better with seven victories with only one loss. Those wins and bonus points for the four falls moved the Cresco Spartans to the top of the team leaderboard going into day two, pursued by West Waterloo and Cedar Rapids.

Friday morning, Rollie woke up with his knee swollen to the size of a grapefruit and was unable to put any weight on his leg. Coach Kilmer reported to the tournament officials Rollie's injury and his inability to continue in the tournament forfeiting his next match as an injury default.

When the quarterfinals round began, the Spartans picked up where they left off the day before. Spider used a first-period takedown and a third-period escape for a 3-1 win, and another loud "BINGO" launched the morning and rallied the crowd.

At 106-pounds, Kent's next contender was an outstanding sophomore from Ames, who placed fourth last year at 98-pounds. He took Kent down in the first period and rode him out. The Ames kid reversed Kent in the second period and dominated Kent for over a minute. The third period started with Kent on the bottom, behind 4-0. He kept trying to stand up for an escape and was repeatedly brought back down to the mat. After a restart with twenty-eight seconds left, instead of a stand-up, Kent hit a switch. The Ames grappler could have easily given up the switch allowing a two-point reversal but instinctively reacted by attempting a re-switch. Kent countered by stepping over his opponent's hips and trapped him on his back for the rest of the period. The Cresco fans screamed with enthusiasm. With two points for the reversal and a three-point near-fall, Kent won 5-4, "BINGO."

Jose wrestled the boy from Eagle Grove he lost to earlier in the year. Jose, being a defensive wrestler on his feet, turned into a takedown machine in the match. He took his victim down and released him only to take him down again and again for a comfortable 9-3 victory and another refrain of "BINGO."

The "BINGO's" continued as Charlie took a first-period lead of 5-0 and hung on to a 6-4 decision. Drew won his match by a score of 6-3 over an admirable competitor from Cedar Falls. At heavyweight, Hoss gave up an escape in the third period but used a well-executed duck-under to pivot behind the Davenport contender. With a tight waist and a heal block, Hoss scored a two-point takedown and rode him out for a 2-1 hard-fought win.

Going into the semi-finals, the Cresco Spartans extended their lead with six wrestlers still in the winner's bracket. Cedar Rapids moved into second place with five competitors in the semis. West Waterloo and Cedar Falls, both advancing four

193

participants, remained in the hunt for a state title.

The Spartans had a chance to distance themselves from the field in the semi-finals with a win at 98. Unable to keep up with the undefeated and returning state runner-up from Cedar Rapids, Spider lost 4-0 to the first of three Cedar Rapids Hornets who qualified for the championship match.

West Waterloo advanced two participants to the finals, both at the expense of the Spartans. The Warhawk 155 pounder schooled Charlie 6-1. Hoss faced the Waterloo heavyweight who beat him easily in the dual meet earlier in the season. It was a closer match, but he ended up on the short end of a 5-2 score.

At 105-pounds, a dominating junior from Mason City used a ferocious cross-face to put Kent in a far-side cradle, pinning him in the third period.

Jose brought the BINGO cards back out with a flawless victory at 127-pounds, winning 7-3. Drew dominated by twice using an armbar and far wrist, rolling his opponent over for near-fall points on his way to the finals with a 10-0 semi-final triumph.

Day two ended as the Cedar Rapids Hornets took the team lead over the Spartans, with West Waterloo a distant third. When the boys were noticeably quiet, heading back to the hotel, Coach Kilmer sensed his guys losing their momentum and brought his brood together in his hotel room.

"You young men set a goal to do something extraordinary and significant for Bing, but it is also important to remember that you are also doing this for yourselves. You will remember this all your lives. It's a two team race between Cedar Rapids and us. We each have six kids still wrestling tomorrow. We have two in the finals and four in the consolations. They have three in the finals and three in the backdoor. All the bonus points for major decisions and pins have kept us in the hunt. Rollie, we needed your pin in your last match, too. That was outstanding and I'm proud of you. Those pin points are what will help us win this thing. We need every point we can get."

Rollie stood on crutches alongside the bed full of wrestlers. Hoss repositioned himself next to Rollie and gave him a gentle pat on the back while the rest of his buddies gave him a little round of applause and saying, "Way to go!" "Good job." "Thanks, Rollie." Rollie bit his lower lip to prevent him from crying. He nodded his head in gratitude.

Coach Kilmer went on, "You guys have done way more than the school, our fans, or your coaches have ever asked of you. But if we are going to do this for Bing, I need you to do even more. The four of you lost tough, tough semi-final matches tonight." Looking directly at Spider, Kent, Charlie, and Hoss.

"The hardest match to prepare for mentally is the first-round tomorrow morning. We call it the Blood Round for a reason. The winner gets a medal and a place on the award stand, while the loser goes home. You guys lost your last matches and are feeling down in the dumps. The kids you paired against are coming off wins in the consolation bracket and feeling rather confident about beating you. It is not going to happen! Get it?" Coach paused and repeated, "Get it?"

The four of them echoed back, "Got it!"

Coach Kilmer unzipped his duffle bag and pulled out a six-inch-tall white plastic toy toilet he received at a white elephant Christmas party when they lived in the twin cities. The guys all snickered. "I need...we need you four to FLUSH away those losses. From this point on, you are thinking about winning your first match tomorrow and seeing yourself on the podium with a third-place medal around your neck."

He held the toy toilet out in his hands. Spider hopped up and turned the lever on the toy toilet, and it made a flushing sound. They all laughed again. Hoss stepped up, followed by Charlie and Kent. Coach again said to each one of them, "Get it?" and they answered, "Got it!"

Coach Hall stepped up, "Bring it in!"

All the wrestlers circled the coaches at the end of the bed and put their hands together. They were waiting for the usual team cheer of 1, 2, 3, Spartans, but unexpectedly Coach Hall sang, "B-I-N-G-O, B-I-N-G-O." They all responded with wide grins, "And Bingo was his name!"

"Now go to bed. Hey, dream about being on the podium, your teammates, championship medallions around your necks, a championship trophy in your arms."

Saturday morning, after weigh-ins, the crew returned to the hotel restaurant for breakfast. The guys joked around with each other. Rollie and Jose put some salt on the table to see who would be the first to get a glass saltshaker to balance on its bottom edge while resting in a small pile of salt. Hoss, Spider, and Drew tried to see who could get a spoon to hang upside-down from the end of their nose. Pete and Charlie were blowing the paper off their straws at each other and laughing. Out of the corner of his eye, Coach Kilmer watched Kent sheepishly unscrewed the top of the glass sugar container, so it laid sitting loose on the top but appeared to be still on the jar. While everyone else was preoccupied, Kent slid it back in front of Hoss.

When the waitress brought their food, she set the plates in front of them. they each replied, "This isn't mine." "Not mine."

Flustered, she kept trying to make sure each kid received the correct order. As soon as she left, they all swapped their plates back to where she initially served them, howling hysterically. Hoss, the instigator, hooted the loudest as he grabbed the sugar jar to pour it on his oatmeal. The sugar lid fell into his oatmeal bowl along with all the sugar in the container. The teenagers erupted one more time. "What the hell!" he shouted, "Umm, sorry, Coach." He eyeballed his peers around the table, attempting

197

to find the guilty prankster. No one fessed up.

Joe, grinning from the escapades happening around the table, whispered to Tom, "Oh, holy moley, they are ready."

The Spartans rolled through the consolation semi-finals with four wins, bookended with pins by Spider and Hoss, and four boisterous "BINGOs." Hoss came off his match with the Cedar Rapids heavyweight and nodded at Coach, "and now they have five." With all four Spartans in the backside bracket making it to the consolation finals, Hoss continued, "Uff Da! How's that for a Blood Round?"

With his parents, aunts, uncles, and cousins in the stands, Charlie added a third-place medal to the Spiegler family legacy. Spider represented his name well, riding his opponent for the entire third period for a nail-biting 1-0 victory to take home a third-place medal. Kent and Hoss picked up fourth place medals putting the Cresco Spartans back on top of the leader board as the tournament headed into the championship finals.

CHAPTER 18

JOSE

The Cedar Rapids Hornets did not back down. They put a finalist in three of the first four weight classes and won two of them. When Jose stepped on the mat, the Hornets commanded a two point team lead. The Spartans needed one more win to capture the state team championship title. Jose's opponent came from Waverly, a familiar foe to Cresco fans, Brad Lentz.

No smack talk this time around from Lentz when the grapplers met in the middle of the inner circle. As he wrapped the green Velcro band around his sock on his left ankle, Lentz eyed Jose up and down. Other than a yellow eight-inch "W" deviation on his back, the undefeated Waverly stud sported all black due to his black tights under his black singlet, and black socks and shoes. Lentz's concentration demonstrated his focus on not underestimating Jose Rodriguez.

The expression on Jose's face never varied

when he stepped on the wrestling mat, but he decided for his last match not to wear tights under his blue singlet. With no socks and bare legs down to his wrestling shoes, he picked up the red band off the mat and put it around his brown ankle.

Tom turned to Joe, "Something wrong with his tights?"

"You don't understand, do ya?" Joe answered. "He's showing it."

"He's showing his legs?" Tom puzzled back.

Joe chuckled at his partner's naivety. "Holy mackerel, you crack me up sometimes. He is showing his brown skin. His pride. Jeez, he is proud to be Hispanic. He is finally goin' to win a tournament. Amazing!"

Tom smiled to himself. "You mean he has been intentionally... well, I'll be damned. What do you know? This is pretty awesome."

The first period began with each grappler alertly positioning and hand-checking with a few half-attempts at takedown shots by both wrestlers to measure their opponent's reaction. Neither combatant made a legitimate shot at penetrating deep underneath. As both wrestlers continued circling, Jose reached for Lentz's head, attempting to tie him up. The referee stopped the match and raised his fist, and pointed with the other hand at Jose.

"Stalling, Red!" he declared, referring to the red ankle band Jose wore. "That's your warning."

Jose did not say a word, just moved back to his center mark to his neutral ready position.

Coach Kilmer and Coach Hall gazed at each other in wonderment.

"What the heck was that?"

Joe uttered back, "Holy cow, I think we're in trouble."

The tempo for both grapplers continued to be methodical and cautious. Lentz shot under Jose on a high double-leg with twenty seconds left, but Jose instinctively sprawled back, threw in a solid cross-face, and Lentz retreated to a neutral stance and circled back to the middle. Jose shadowed him, and as they squared up, the referee stopped the match and raised his fist again.

"Stalling, Red. One point, Green!"

Coach Kilmer stood up from his corner chair in disbelief and moved towards the scoring table. The referee pointed at him. "Sit down, Coach! Your wrestler is not attacking."

Tom returned to his chair, and the match continued. Jose hit a fireman's carry to Lentz's right side with five seconds left in the period. A masterful shot with his head deep under the arm, his left hand locked on Lentz's elbow, and his right arm high between the legs. A textbook fireman's carry. Controlling from both knees underneath Lentz, Jose dumped him over his head to the mat. Lentz tried to scramble to his base as Jose climbed onto his hips. The buzzer rang, and the Cresco crowd sprang to

201

their feet! 2-1, Jose!

The referee waved his hands, crossing his arms back and forth in front of his face. "No points! Time was up before control." Some "boos" streamed down from the Cresco stands as the Spartan fans identified Jose's takedown. Even the silence of the Waverly coaches and fans indicated they sensed a lucky call. A belief grew within the coaching pair in the Spartans' corner regarding this referee's motive.

The second period began with Lentz in the down position. He immediately hit an effective inside leg stand-up, turned, and came right back at Jose with a single-leg shot. Jose countered, pushed Lentz's head to the outside, and reached across to Lentz's far leg into a switch position. He finished by turning the corner, back on top of Lentz. Lentz re-established his base as they landed out of bounds.

To Tom, Joe, and the Cresco fans, Lentz scored an escape point, and Jose secured a takedown for two points. The referee signaled no points.

Tom approached the scoring bench along with the referee. Tom pressed him, "It shoulda been an escape and then a takedown."

"Not as I saw it, Coach. No change in control. Green is still down. Tell your little Mexican to work for a pin, or I'll nail him for stalling again."

Tom's jaw dropped. He could not believe he just heard the referee call Jose a little Mexican.

202

Returning to his coaching chair at the corner of the mat, he shared what he just heard with his assistant coach. Joe just shook his head.

Jose rode Lentz for forty seconds before Lentz escaped for a point. The second period ended with Lentz leading 2-0.

Jose started the third period in the down position. With Lentz on top of him, Jose hit a series of three short sit-outs, setting up Lentz as he tried to track Jose. Lentz got too high over Jose's shoulders, and Jose turned back underneath Lentz into a fireman's carry position again. When he dumped Lentz to his back, he trapped his arm, catching Lentz exposed to near-fall criteria. He held Lentz for three seconds before Lentz twisted his arm away from Jose, rolled to his stomach, and pushed back to his base.

The coaches and fans were on their feet cheering for a two-point reversal and at least two near-fall points, if not three. The referee signaled two points for the reversal but gave no near-fall points. With a 2-2 tie, Jose controlled Lentz with an ankle hook and two-on-one wrists ride.

The referee stopped the match with less than forty seconds to go. "Stalling, Red! You're not working for a pin. One Point, Green."

Kilmer stood in protest, but it would not make a difference to go to the scorer's table. Now behind 3-2, Coach signaled to Jose to let Lentz go by flipping the back of his hands away. At the whistle,

Jose pushed Lentz away, giving him a one-point escape. Jose needed a takedown to tie the match and go to overtime. For thirty seconds, Jose attacked Lentz relentlessly. Brad Lentz's experience surfaced as he wrestled extremely smart with a two point lead, staying in a skillful defensive position, refusing to tie up, and kept his distance while protecting his legs. He would even be willing to accept a warning for stalling or even a penalty point, but it never came. The lens of this referee blurred his perception of stalling. The match ended with Lentz winning 4-2.

The foes met at the starting points and shook hands. The referee raised Lentz's hand as the winner and state champion. Jose turned to the referee, as he always does, "Gracias por arbitrar mi Partido."

The referee, outraged by Jose's comment, clutched him by the upper arm and marched him over to the Cresco coaches. The startled coaches stared at the referee, wondering what now.

"This little wetback just spoke to me in Spanish, and I want to know what he said."

Coach Hall began to explain what Jose says at the end of each match, but Tom interrupted, "Take your hands off my kid. I'll tell you what he said. YOU'RE a racist son-of-a-bitch and have no business refereeing!"

The referee released Jose's arm, made a "T" with his hands, and angrily fired back, "That's a flagrant foul, and that'll cost you one team point!"

Kilmer did not even argue as the referee left to report the loss of one team point to the official table.

"Lo siento, Coach, it's not what I told him."

"I know, but it felt REALLY good to tell him what I thought. I'm sorry he cost you a fair shake at the state title."

Jose smiled, "Gracias."

Brad Lentz came jogging back across the mat to Jose and gave him a gentle bear hug. Stumbling with the words he rehearsed, Lentz exclaimed, "Gracias por luchar conmigo. usted es un buen luchador y oponente campeón." He shook Jose's hand one more time before shaking both Cresco coaches' hands. Lentz jogged back across the mat to his coaches.

"What did he tell you?"

"He thanked me for wrestling him and said I was a good wrestler and champion opponent."

Lentz's classy action caught Coach Kilmer off guard, forcing him to concentrate on reserving his emotions as he recalled coaching this fine young man all season, "I'll be damned. You know what? He is so absolutely right!" Holding Jose's head against his chest, he hugged him like a father hugs his son. "Gracias, Jose Rodriquez."

Jose hugged him back. "Thanks for believing in me, Coach."

Tom gave a thumbs up to the Waverly coach with his arms still around Jose, who nodded back.

205

Coach turned and stood side by side with Jose, with one arm around Jose's shoulders. The pair faced the Cresco fans in the stands allowing them to acknowledge the accomplishment of this Hispanic United States teenage citizen from Cresco, Iowa. The crowd responded with a round of applause, but when Coach raised Jose's hand high into the air, the clapping turned into a thunderous standing cheer of "BINGO."

Jose raised his head high as he caught a glimpse of his proud mother and father standing next to Charlie's parents. In a great act of compassion, Ron Peckham had recruited a milking crew from several of his dairy farmer friends to do the chores and milking shifts at the Spiegler farm. Ron understood the significance of watching his son wrestle and gave Arturo and Rosie cash for traveling, lodging, and attending the state tournament so they could see their son's achievement. It was the first time Cresco fans saw Jose smile after a match.

CHAPTER 19

CHAMPIONSHIP

Algona's Steve Kalen, considered the top 185-pounder not only in the state of Iowa but in the entire country, officially signed a letter of intent to wrestle for Cresco native Dr. Harold Nichols and the Iowa State Cyclones. Kalen, the defending state champion at 185-pounds, had been the runner-up at 167-pounds in his sophomore year. He had a career record of eighty-six victories with only four losses. Undefeated this season entering the championship match, he had compiled eighteen falls, giving up only one takedown.

The Cresco coaches and Drew spent a portion of the day trying to strategize but were unable to plan out a scheme. Drew had never wrestled Kalen, and the Algona Bulldog pinned his way to the championship match, limited their ability to scout him in live situations to identify any weaknesses. Drew would have to wrestle a flawless six minutes, find a way to take him down somehow, score an escape, and then be able to hold him down.

Back in Cresco, the local radio station broadcasted the state tournament matches live. Wrestling fans packed Tuchek's Tavern, drinking Hamm's and Budweiser beer and listening intensely together to the radio announcer's play-by-play. The radio crackled, "Casey Prine, live from the Vet Auditorium in Des Moines. The 1973 state wrestling championship has come down to the 185-pound match. While crowning two individual state champions, one at 98 and the other at 119, the Cedar Rapids Hornets have a two-point lead for the team title. Oops, make that a three-point lead after we lost a team point for some reason at the end of Jose's 127-pound match. We can only assume Coach Kilmer offended the referee at the end that heartbreaking loss."

"It doesn't matter if it's two or three points. If Drew Parker wins this match, Cresco will pick up four additional team points. For the Spartans to be crowned state champions, it will be up to Drew to, somehow, do the impossible and defeat the defending state champion, Steve Kalen of Algona. But the wrestling fans of Cresco know, if anyone can come through for the Spartans, it is Drew Parker. And here we go. Kalen has the red ankle band to go with his red singlet with Algona blazed in black on his chest. In his blue Cresco singlet and tights with the large "C" on his back, Parker is wearing the green band. They shake hands, and we're ready to wrestle."

For the two minutes of the first period, the warriors went at it. Neither wrestler stopped moving, pushing, jamming, tying up, circling, shooting, blocking, adjusting elevation, countering, squaring up. Each grappler took one deep shot during the round. Drew hit a low single, trapping Kalen's leg, and elevated it to his waist. The Bulldog grappler turned 180 degrees and kicked himself free. Kalen shot in on a high single leg on the edge of the circle, and Drew hooked in a Whizzer, used his leverage to prevent control as he sprawled back, going out of bounds. Period one ended with no score, 0-0.

Drew won the coin flip and deferred the choice to the third period. Kalen chose the down position to begin the second period. Coach Kilmer had seen Drew dominate accomplished wrestlers before and hoped he could ride this opponent the entire second period. It did not come close to happening. Kalen popped right up, blocked Drew's attempt to under hook him from behind, and then controlled Drew's tight waist hand and peeled it off. Kalen turned his hips, lowered his elevation, and faced him. Drew immediately released him, giving him a one-point escape. But as he circled back to the middle of the mat, he made a mistake when he overreacted to a partial shot by Kalen and ended up on his knees with his head below him. The Algona senior instantly trapped Drew in a front headlock. As

Drew turned, trying to gain his balance on his feet and push his foe by, Kalen shucked him up and shot a double leg. He picked Drew up in the air and dropped him for a textbook two-point takedown. Drew fought to his base and, with twenty seconds left in the second period, climbed to his feet and fought for a one-point escape. Period two ended with Drew behind 3-1.

The third period began with Drew choosing the down position. He needed a reversal for two points to tie or an escape and takedown for the lead. When the whistle blew, Kalen hit a spiral ride with a hard under hook and thigh pry, keeping the pressure on Drew's front shoulder preventing him from popping up to his feet. The dominance on the top continued for over a minute and a half. Each time Drew attempted a stand-up, Kalen countered and drove him back to the mat. With seventeen seconds left, the Algona wrestler drove Drew of bounds resulting in a restart at the center circle.

Instead of standing up on the whistle, Drew rolled a short sit-out and flipped his hips, putting Kalen out of position for his spiral ride. Drew promptly executed a Granby roll, popped to his feet, and faced Kalen. The one-point escape left Drew one point behind at 3-2. Kalen immediately attempted to push Drew away, but Drew did not back out and locked onto Kalen's wrist with his opposite hand. He short dragged it by, shot right back underneath to a high crotch, turned the corner, and drove the Bulldog to the mat for a two-point takedown.

In unison, a roar shattered the stillness in Tuchek's Tavern in response to the narrative on the radio.

"Takedown! Takedown for Drew! Two points! He is ahead 4-3 with five seconds left. Kalen has jumped to his feet. Drew is trying to hold on. Kalen's turning, sprawling. One-point escape!"

When Kalen sprawled out, Drew attempted to hang on with his arm around his hip, fighting the leverage. He heard a pop in his shoulder and felt the pain as it popped out of the socket. Before he could shout out, Kalen attacked with a front under hook driving Parker over to his back, but time ran out. At the whistle, Parker ended up landing on his injured shoulder with his opponent's weight on top of him. No takedown. With the escape, Kalen tied the score 4-4. When Drew's shoulder hit the mat, somehow it slipped back into place, but something else went incredibly wrong as intense pain burst throughout his shoulder. He could not elevate his arm or even raise his hand off the mat.

Drew laid back on the mat and did not move. The referee announced, "Going to sudden death overtime. First to score wins. Let's go!" Then he saw the pain on Drew's face and called the Cresco coaches over and waved for the tournament doctor.

As the doctor came to the mat, the referee met with him and described how the injury

211

occurred. When Coach Kilmer began to discuss what happened with the doctor, Parker rolled over, pushed himself up with his functional arm, and bounced to his feet.

The doctor moved towards Drew, "Okay, let me see your shoulder. I need to examine it."

"The heck you will. Get away from me." Drew walked towards his coaches' chairs at the corner of the mat.

The doctor turned to Coach Kilmer, who motioned with his head for the doctor to leave. He did. Coach trailed Drew to the chairs in the corner of the mat. The referee came over to their corner, notified the group, and let them know the scoring table had initiated the injury time clock. Tom consoled Drew as Joe began taping his shoulder.

"Not good. Something is wrong here." Hearing his wife's insistent voice in his head prompting him to remember people being more important. "You gave it your best shot, Drew. It has been a great run to get here. We're done. It's okay to let it go. It's over. I'm scared for you."

Staring up in the air, "No, it's not over until I say it's over! It's not for me, not you, not Cresco. It's for Bingo." He paused and then quietly mumbled, "and... I'm scared, too, Coach, but this... it's for my dad. He would tell me it's okay to be scared, but the job's gotta get done."

With the focus on the post-season and Bingo on everyone's mind, Coach Kilmer neglected to address the emotional drain on Drew with the loss of his father. Drew continued to stare at the rafters in 'The Barn.' The Spartan wrestling coaches exchanged depressed glances and shook their heads sideways in a "how could we have forgotten this" look. Tom choked back a tear as he reached over with the back of his fingers and gently rubbed Drew's cheek as Coach Hall worked on his shoulder. Drew took a deep breath, dropped his chin down towards his chest, and relaxed in response to the loving touch of his coach.

Suddenly, Drew broke the awkward silence between the three of them as he turned his head to Coach Hall, "Dang it, Hall. You're taping the wrong shoulder."

Coach Hall kept taping and answered, "Yup, I know, and, holy cow, I'm doing a terrific job of it."

Drew and Coach Kilmer traded puzzled looks as if they were asking each other, is he saying what I think he's saying? Coach Hall kept murmuring, "There's nothing left, man. You can't shoot or defend yourself against this guy without your left arm. So, we either quit or try to tempt him to shoot to your good arm and see what happens."

Still stumped, Drew asked both coaches, "Do you think it'll work?"

Before Tom replied, Coach Hall exclaimed, "Heck, no!" They all three chuckled through the tension of the moment. The humor in Coach Hall's answer helped Drew forget the agony and throbbing in his other shoulder for the moment.

The referee moved over to the Algona coaches. He did not expect Drew to continue as they watched across the mat as Coach Hall finished taping up Drew's shoulder. Drew turned to the mat.

"Hey, they're going to go," the referee uttered over his shoulder as he shuffled to the middle of the mat. "Let's do it!"

The Algona head coach advised his wrestler, "listen, let's not mess around here, take a hard-low single under his bad arm and finish it in a hurry." He smiled, "then we can go have a steak dinner and celebrate."

Back in Cresco, the radio resumed, "Live from Des Moines Veterans Auditorium and the finals at 185-pounds. Drew Parker turned what appeared like a sure defeat with ten seconds to go into what would have been an unbelievable victory to only have it tied back up at the whistle. On top of giving up the tying point, it appears Drew has severely injured his right shoulder. This is not good, folks! Drew is at the corner of the mat, getting his shoulder taped by Coach Hall. Coach Kilmer gives him some last-second advice as he is snapping Drew's headgear in place for him. Drew is going back out. Here we go."

The only sound in the Tuchek's Tavern belonged to Casey Prine on the radio, "Drew is now slowly going to the circle. His right shoulder is taped across the top down the front. The white athletic

214

tape winds around to his shoulder blade. His upper arm is taped to his body, so he cannot move it. Drew steps forward onto the red line. He is leaning slightly at the hip with his knees bent. His hands are at his sides. Not a particularly impressive stance. I hate to say it, but it's all he has left."

"Steve Kalen bends forward over his lead knee keeping his head up and his hands out front protecting his front leg. He is certainly in an aggressive stance. The referee has stepped in between the two wrestlers and is saying something to Drew. Drew glances at him and nods. The referee puts his whistle in his mouth, steps back, and extends his hand out front. He gives a quick jerk of his hand and blows his whistle."

Drew did not move. The Algona wrestler did a quick elevation change, lowering himself even more as he took a long step. Driving to his forward knee, he attacked Drew's right leg and Drew sprawled his leg back. The tape ripped away from his arm and shoulder as he brought his right hand up, cupped it, chopped down on the back of Kalen's head, driving it down towards the mat. Kalen, caught by surprise, was expecting little if any resistance from what he thought was Drew's injured arm. He ended up on his elbows and knees and tried to regain his position in front of Drew. Drew's continued pressure on Kalen's head forced Kalen's weight to remain on his hands as he attempted to push himself back up. It was just long enough to prevent him from reaching up to stop Drew from spinning around to the left. Drew landed behind his adversary, coming down on his near ankle, with his chest and head in the middle of Kalen's back. With his right hand, he threw a tight waist across his foe's stomach.

With his left arm drooped down, he held Kalen as tightly as he could with one arm. The Bulldog exploded up, turned, and faced him, ready to attack. The whistle blew. The referee held two fingers in the air, and the match ended. Steve Kalen dropped to his knees, sat back on his ankles, put his chin down on his chest, and locked his fingers behind his neck in disbelief.

Drew fell to his back and closed his eyes. For a minute, he did not move, and the world seemed blank. He heard no noise, and all he could feel was his heart beating. With the sweat running down his cheek, his father's presence began to sweep over him; a wonderful and peaceful feeling. Content to lay there forever, Drew sensed his dad calling his name, and tears began to swell up in Drew's eyes. "Drew, Drew, it's okay."

"Dad!"

"You did it!" Drew opened his eyes. Coach Kilmer gently touched his face, wiped the sweat and tears away. "You did it! You're a state champion. And so is Bingo!"

The noise and cheers resonated now, but he wasn't ready to celebrate just yet. He knew Kalen outwrestled him for all but the last fifteen seconds, and then he stole the championship in overtime. He also knew he did what he had to do and the job got done.

Coach unsnapped Drew's headgear and Drew turned to push himself up but could not. With no spring in his step now, he appreciated the coach helping him up. He glanced at Steve Kalen, who remain centered on the mat, sitting on his ankles with his head down. Both gladiators had spent it all, physically and emotionally. The battle complete, Drew ambled over and dropped in front of his foe, mirroring his position. Kalen lifted his chin, and the two of them made eye contact. Kalen reached out with his hand at chest level and Drew matched him. Using an athlete's handshake, wrapping thumbs, they shook hands. A hush swept the auditorium as all eyes converged on the two counterparts in the midpoint of the arena. Kalen stood, still holding Drew's hand, helped the new champion to his feet.

The silence gradually rolled over to a thunder of a standing ovation for both wrestlers with respect for their effect and sportsmanship. The referee took Drew's hand from Kalen and raised it in victory. The Cresco fans exploded with repeated shouts of "BINGO," but it did not stop. The roars of "BINGO" grew louder and louder as wrestling fans throughout "The Barn" joined in to acknowledge the incredible victory and the story of Bing Natvig. BINGO cards were thrown into the air by fans in

217

celebration. Lori Kilmer sat next to Drew's mother, Karla Parker. They both burst into tears, and they hugged each other in jubilation.

The "BINGO" shouts continued as Pete, Spider, Kent, Charlie, Jose, and Hoss joined Rollie on his crutches and the cheerleaders at the edge of the mat to greet Drew. The shouts swiftly transformed to the chant of "State Champs" clap, clap, "State Champs" clap, clap...over and over. Drew finally smiled. He eyed his buddies as they gathered around him. "We did it! Bingo is a state champion!"

Coach Kilmer stood next to his boys but faced the crowd. With tears of elation in his eyes, Tom combed the stands for his wife. When they finally made eye contact, Lori waved and blew him a kiss. He raised both arms in triumph and grinned at her. He gradually turned back and joined his assistant coach and his wrestlers in celebration.

The chant carried over to Tuchek's Tavern. The patrons pounded on the bar, raised their glasses high in celebration, and clanged their glasses in a toast. Beer flew all over, including on each other, but no one seemed to care. It seemed as if every home in Cresco echoed the cheer of "State Champs" as youngsters stepped outside their houses, beating pots and pans with spoons. Even the sounds of some firecrackers exploded across the town. The chant of "State Champs" echoed down the intensive care unit hallway at the Mayo Clinic in Rochester, Minnesota.

When the team took the podium for the trophy presentation, each qualifier and coach received a championship gold medallion on a red and white lanyard. With his lanyard around his neck, Coach Kilmer smiled, showing the pride and love he had for these kids. But he could not prevent his smile from turning to a huge grin as he thought about Wes Sorenson getting to have the words 'State Champions' sewn on the back of his letterman's jacket.

CHAPTER 20
BUS

In the early morning March darkness, the Main Street Diner sign needed a new fluorescent bulb on its bottom half as it sputtered on and off. The small blue Greyhound Bus logo within the silhouette of a silver greyhound dog hung by two small chains beneath the café sign. Spider and his mother barely noticed it as they walked down the sidewalk. Although it was March, most of the snow had disappeared off the streets and sidewalks. The large piles of snow the city snow removers stacked tall during the winter remained on edges of parking lots and driveways but had melted down to tiny heaps of a version of dirty colored snow mixed with dirt and sand. The pair delicately stepped over the slush of water, and snow pooled at the sidewalk curbing when they came to a street crossing.

The temperature dropped into the high twenties but consistently warmed up well above freezing when the sun rose. It still felt warm in comparison to the long cold winter they just experienced. The mother and son walked the eight blocks from their house without much to say to each other. Sadie wore her cotton floral church dress with her twenty-some-year-old grey wool winter coat over the top. Wearing a red scarf and a pair of knitted mittens, she carried a small brown and tan plaid suitcase in one hand and her purse in the other. Spider dressed in his Cresco wrestling sweatshirt, a pair of worn Levi's with holes in one knee, a black stocking cap, dirty cream-colored high-top Pro-Keds tennis shoes, and a pair of brown cotton work gloves. His father's Army green drawstring knapsack was draped over his left shoulder and a scuffed up canvas duffle bag dangled from his right hand.

As they arrived at the Main Street Diner, the pair noticed Pastor Johansen through the glass door. Coach Kilmer initiated a conversation with the pastor a week earlier, eliciting his support for Spider and his mother. The pastor, dressed in all black with the traditional white rectangle exposed at the front of his clerical collar, leaned on the glass countertop next to the cash register waiting for Tony, the diner's owner, to hang up the telephone.

Spider peered down the street and then opened the door for his mother. Contrasting Pastor Johansen's apparel, Tony's all-white appearance included a stained white apron around his neck, tied around his waist partially covered his dull white t-shirt and white slacks. Spider watched Tony wipe his hands on the bottom of his apron, pick up an envelope with the Greyhound Bus logo on it, and hand it to the clergyman.

"There ya go, Reverend. I called dispatch in Decorah. The driver knows he has a 'pick up' for two riders this morning. It should be here in fifteen minutes or so. Good morning, Sadie. Hi, Spider." Tony acknowledged the new arrivals. "Congratulations on placing at state. Boy, a big "WOW" for a freshman."

Before either answered, Tony turned and shuffled down to the end of the counter. His coffee cup sat in front of a trio of his regular cronies occupying the last three stools next to the kitchen. He snatched the glass coffee pot off the warmer on his way by and topped off each of their coffees. They resumed their conversation as if it had never been interrupted, paying no attention to the three people at the front of the café. The rest of the breakfast crowd would not be straggling in for another hour.

An off-white Formica countertop with stains and cigarette burns extended from the cash counter to the kitchen wall of the long, narrow café. Thirteen pedestal stools topped by red-leathered round seats anchored in a line in front of the counter. Most of the leather seat tops sported small slashes or holes. One stool was missing when Tony removed it after the pedestal broke off the base. He plans on having it re-welded, but it's been nearly three years. It is a sore spot with his wife, Susie, who reminds Tony once a week to fix it.

The checkerboard of black and white vinyl tile floor from the 1950s could only be identifiable in small areas of the café. Over time, Tony swapped out damaged black tiles with cheaper regular stock white ones. Four booths with high back benches lined down the right wall. The black leather on the bench seats had long ago worn through and was browner in spots than black.

Susie commanded the kitchen and made sure the café remained spotlessly clean despite its age. She was known for her mouth-watering meals, and Spider and Sadie smelled the fantastic aroma of fresh cinnamon rolls baking in the café ovens.

"Good morning, you guys!" Pastor Johansen greeted the pair and escorted them to the first booth.

Spider moved in front of his mother to make sure he sat in the booth with a full view of the front door. "Morning, Pastor," Spider spoke as he took off his cap and gloves and shook Pastor Johannsen's hand.

Sadie set her suitcase on the floor next to the bench and took a seat opposite Spider. She put her purse, mittens, and scarf on the table between them. "Good Mornin', Reverend. I don't know how to thank you for your help. We'll repay you someday."

Pastor Johansen remained standing, leaning

on the top of the high back of Spider's bench seat, and replied, "Don't worry about it, Sadie. It's your church. We love doing the Lord's work for him. He asked us to take care of you. Here we are, and here are your tickets." He handed Sadie the Greyhound envelope. "You will get on the westbound bus here shortly. You will need to get off at Davis Corners and wait for the bus going north to Rochester. It should not be too long of a wait...ten minutes at most. When you get to Rochester, the bus driver will take a break for thirty minutes, but it's the same bus going on to Minneapolis. If you want, you can get off for a while, take a break, and get back on...or just wait on the bus. I called your daughter, Ellie, in Minneapolis, and she knows you are arriving at 10:40. She will be there to pick you up."

He smiled and continued, "I think we're set! Can we pray?" He put his hand on Spider's shoulder. Sadie and Spider folded their hands on the tabletop. "Oh, Lord..."

"Oh, crap!" Spider blurted out as his dad stepped in through the café's front door.

Ken Westby came strutting into the café. "Well, well, well, look what I found. What the hell do you think you little pee brains are up to? Sneaking out in the dark of the frickin' night with a suitcase and MY knapsack?" His right arm, in a white cast from his hand to his shoulder, bent at ninety degrees at his elbow. A sling hung down from around his neck to support the cast, and his face

225

disclosed some previous bruising. He wore the same pair of greasy cotton work pants for over a week with his scuffed up brown work boots and a soiled white t-shirt with the right armhole torn open to fit his cast through. Crooked on his head was a filthy mesh baseball-style cap faded red with sweat stains and a yellow Garst Seed Corn emblem on the front. His eyes matched his cap, and Spider was sure his father was still half drunk. "I've come to get my shit back, start'n with my wife." He moved toward Sadie.

Pastor Johansen moved forward to step between Ken and Sadie, but Spider stood up and put his hand on the pastor's chest to stop him. Spider stepped out of the booth and towards his father.

"What the hell is this? Little Spider gets a medal, thinks he can take his old man now. Just 'cause I got a cast on doesn't mean I can't pound the shit out of you with it, you little dick head."

"Cast or no cast, your days of hurt'n mom are done. And yeah, cast or no cast, I CAN take you if I have to!" Spider inched forward. Surprisingly, Ken backed up a step with an awkward pause.

Susie came running out of the kitchen with a white paper sack in each hand. At the same time, they heard the sound of air brakes from the bus pulling up in front of the café. Susie stepped between Ken and Spider and set the sacks on the table in front of Sadie.

"There ya go, Miss Sadie. Two cartons of milk and two fresh warm cinnamon rolls for your trip. On the house. Tony's and my pleasure." The pair thanked her as she turned to Ken and pointed to the door, "Now you get the hell out of my diner, Ken Westby!"

Ken glared at Spider and then at Sadie. He mumbled something, but they only heard, "Good riddance to the two of you." He turned and walked out the front door.

Susie rolled her eyes up towards the ceiling, took a deep breath, and then turned to Pastor Johansen, "Sorry 'bout my language, Reverend! But I should have said that years ago."

The pastor answered, "Me, too!"

Sadie giggled a bit as the pastor's response broke the tension and brought smiles to each one. Spider did not remember the last time he heard his mother laugh. It put a broad grin on his face. Susie bent down and hugged Sadie around the neck and gave her a little peck on the cheek. "Take care, you guys," pinching Spider's cheek and giving him a wink as she walked by him on her way back to the kitchen.

Peeking back over her shoulder, Susie smiled and nodded at the pastor, "You're a good man, Reverend."

Sadie stood, slid out of the booth, and hugged Pastor Johansen, "Thank you!"

The pastor answered, "You betcha! Now you take care, Sadie. And the Lord be with you, Jan!"

"Jan..." Spider thought to himself. He liked it. He put on his stocking cap, gloves and collected his

227

bags as his mother slipped on her mittens and wrapped her scarf around her neck. The pastor picked up her suitcase. Sadie carried the white sacks with the milk and cinnamon rolls along with her purse, and they walked out the door. Spider went first, checking up and down the street to make sure his father had left. A sense of relief could be seen in their faces as they walked towards the bus. Sadie handed the bus driver their tickets. The driver punched the tickets, returned them to her, and took the bags. He slid them into the underneath compartment as Sadie and Spider climbed the steps into the silver and blue bus and conveyed their goodbyes to the pastor.

Unexpectedly a vehicle pulled in behind the Greyhound bus. As Spider reached the aisle at the top of the bus steps, he heard someone calling out his name. Spider search the sidewalk edge through the bus window underneath the luggage rack, afraid he might see his father again. Tom Kilmer walked along the side of the bus, staring up into the dark windows from the outside, "Spider, Spider!"

Spider turned around, climbed back down the bus's steps, and found Tom asking the bus driver a question. Spider leaped down on both feet to the pavement, "What are you doing here, Coach?"

Diverting his attention away from the bus driver, "I couldn't let you go without wishing you good luck and saying goodbye. I have a present for you." As the coach reached in his pocket, he continued, "You're moving to my old fishing territory, and who knows, you might turn into a fisherman. You'll need this."

Coach Kilmer pulled out a small yellow plastic case with a clear top and handed it to Spider. Through the lid, Spider spied the Muddler Fishing Fly sitting on a grey foam pad. "Coach, it's the fishing fly your dad gave you when you were a kid."

"I know. I will always remember the day he gave it to me. Now I'll always remember the day I gave it to you."

"I can't take this." Spider fought hard to suppress his tears.

"It's what fathers do. They pass on a piece of their heart."

Spider, who has always guarded his emotions, unexpectedly wrapped his arms around his coach and planted his head on the coach's shoulder. Through his now watery eyes, he uttered something he never spoke out loud to anyone before, "Love ya, Coach."

"Love you, too, Spider," Coach Kilmer whispered in Spider's ear as he cradled his head and returned the hug.

CHAPTER 21
SHERIFF

The sheriff's office and county jail, built in 1882, sits across the parking lot behind the Howard County Courthouse on Main Street. The county jailor lives in the residential apartment above the office of the red brick building. Extending from the sheriff's office was the single-level wing containing a small booking office and a booking cell. Behind a steel door off of the booking office ran a short corridor consisting of five-barred jail cells.

Sheriff John Haley sat on his wheeled oak office chair, wary not to lean back too far and end up on the floor with his heels in the air. He knew this from experience. Though he owned multiple sets, he always dressed the same when on duty with his issued uniform of brown pants and a neatly pressed tan shirt with a dark brown tie. The gold Howard County Sheriff patch emblazed the shoulder of his left shirt sleeve. He took time every morning to polish his brown rounded toe cowboy boots, his belt buckle with the county emblem, and his badge with SHERIFF boldly imprinted across the top above his name.

The sheriff's formal hat, a brown campaign-style hat with a stiff brim and a gold star on the front, was displayed neatly on the wooden file cabinet next to his desk. A few years ago, he convinced the county board of supervisors to allow his deputies and him to wear brown baseball-style mesh caps with the sheriff patch on the front. The patch matched the one on their shirt sleeves. His cap hung on a hook on the wall next to his sheriff jacket and black leather gun belt. His simple gun belt held his Smith & Wesson Model 10 revolver in a holster, an ammunition pouch, a black lacquered nightstick, and a set of silver handcuffs.

Sheriff Haley wrestled for the Spartans and placed fourth in the state in 1952. Built like Spider in high school, though taller and heavier, the sheriff never considered himself an intimidating specimen. In the early 1960s, when "The Andy Griffith Show" became popular on television, his appearance earned him the nickname "Barney Fife." It did not bother him because most people in the county held tremendous respect for him, partially because of his "wrestling fame" but primarily because of his ability to defuse situations.

His natural ability to convey empathy and think on his feet for peaceful resolutions got him elected Sheriff of Howard County in 1964 after serving as a deputy for ten years. Still fit but forty pounds heavier than his high school wrestling weight, the sheriff has outwrestled more than a few guys. Other than at the shooting range, he has only drawn his pistol six times in the line of duty in nearly eighteen years of police service, firing it only once into the air to stop a suspect from running away.

The sheriff spun around away from his desk to put a report into the file. Glancing out the window, he saw a shiny white and blue Ford with police lights on the top pull into the courthouse parking lot. The sheriff did not need to see the INS golden logo on the car door to know exactly who was in the car and why they were in Cresco. With their Midwest regional office in St. Paul, Minnesota, the US Immigration and Naturalization Services Program Division agents oversee detention and deportation. Sheriff Haley had not seen a federal agent in town in nearly two years but had a pretty reasonable suspicion on what brought them here. He assumed they had some urgency on this trip to be here early in the morning. Sheriff Haley calmly thumbed through his Rolodex and then picked up his rotary telephone and dialed.

Haley remained on the phone as the door opened, and the two INS officers stepped into the sheriff's office. He recognized the shorter but higher ranking of the two. The sheriff worked with him on three other occasions and respected him for treating people with dignity.

233

The Iowa countryside required plenty of farm work but not as labor-intensive as the west and the southwest United States, where harvesting by hand was far more prevalent. Many Iowa farmers employed what they referred to as hired hands who helped with their daily operation. Some of these farmers provided housing for their hands. Occasionally, a migrant farmworker emerged working for a local farmer. Sooner or later, a report came into the sheriff's office, which obligated the sheriff to contact the federal immigration agency. He often encouraged the farmer to have the worker move on or convince the farmer to let him go. A county sheriff had no authority to ask for proof of citizenship or the ability to detain anyone. Even if he did, he was not sure what he would do with them. If they stayed on too long, the Feds came in and picked them up.

Sheriff Haley continued on the phone and gave the agents a thumbs up, acknowledging their arrival. The senior agent nodded his head, smiled, and return a little "gun" wave with his index finger and thumb. The other agent appeared to be a little annoyed as he waited for the small-town sheriff.

"I know Annie, times have changed. You just cannot trust people like you used to. Yes, Annie, I will be out shortly. Not as soon as I would like. A couple of important agents just walked in my door, and they will need my attention first." The sheriff smiled at the agents and continued on the phone.

234

"Okay, but I am afraid it's the way it's going to be. I know. We'll get it solved. Bye now, Annie."

"Hello, Agent Stewart. It has been a while. How are you?"

"Nice to see you, John. I am doing fine. You know, we go back far enough for you to call me Carl. This is Agent Jack Booth. Jack, this is Sheriff John Haley."

The sheriff stood up, walked to the counter, exchanged handshakes and greetings with the men. He offered them coffee, but neither agent took him up on it after their brief inspection of the old silver dented coffee percolator sitting on the end of the counter. The sheriff refilled his cup and sat back down at his desk.

"For city boys, Carl, you guys must have gotten up awful early this morning to be here by now. How was the drive?"

Agent Stewart chuckled. "Glad I have a young buck with me today so he could do the driving while I took a catnap on the way down." He continued, "Stopped at the Rusty Rail in Rochester for a little road trip breakfast, and here we are."

"Did ya have the biscuits and gravy?" The sheriff inquired, but the junior agent, clearing his throat, interrupted the personal conversation.

Sheriff Haley turned his attention to the younger man. "I can only assume what brings you here. Do you have a name?"

The junior agent pulled out a small black

spiral notebook and, without a smile, flipped through a few pages. "Greg Spi. S-P-I-E-G-L-E-R." Spelling it out as he realized he probably would not pronounce it correctly. "We have an anonymous tip of an illegal immigrant, a Mexican, working on his farm."

Sheriff Haley replied, "Well, it's pronounced SpEE-gler. Greg has 360 acres six miles south of town on the other side of the Turkey River. He farms mostly corn, soybeans, and pasture, but he expanded his dairy operation earlier last year and hired a Mexican hand experienced with milking. I heard he moved on with the first snowfall. The farm is a little tricky to find because you must wind around after crossing the Vernon Springs Bridge. Hey Carl, I need to head south anyway in response to that phone call. Do you want me to take you out there?"

"We would appreciate it. That would be great. Okay with you, Jack?" The agents eyeballed each other, and the younger one shrugged his shoulders. "We are in a little bit of a hurry. If we pick up any illegals, we will head back to St. Paul. Otherwise, we are going on to Postville when we finish here."

Sheriff Haley headed toward the back room, "I gotta take a leak. There's another restroom over to the left if you boys need one."

Both agents moved across the room. The sheriff took his time in the back and then reappeared, slowly putting on his sheriff jacket along with his gun belt as the Federal agents waited patiently. The trio headed out the front door, and the sheriff locked the door behind them. Walking single file on the sidewalk around to the back of the jailhouse, they climbed the four steps up to the courthouse parking lot.

"Looks like you need to wash your car, Sheriff." The junior agent made fun of the sheriff's car caked in yellow limestone dust. Someone had written 'WASH ME' in the dirt on the trunk. The sheriff was a little embarrassed by the message because he usually keeps his patrol car spotless. But he smiled to himself, knowing the little road trip he would be taking them on will make it unmistakably easy for a 'WASH ME' note to end up on the trunk of their shiny blue car.

Sheriff Haley took the lead with his green-colored patrol car as the INS officers tailed him down Main Street. At the point Highway 9 meets the Protivin Road, he took the diagonal gravel road and headed south to Vernon Springs, where the Turkey River spills over a small dam and flows under a wooden framed one-lane bridge. They slowly crossed the bridge, which rattled the cars as they bounced over the uneven planks forming the bridge floor. Both cars climbed up the gradual hill on the other side.

At the top of the hill, the sheriff turned left onto a less maintained side road, winding above the river for a mile. Sheriff Haley drove a little faster than he usually drove on a rutted "washboard" road, even as it caused his car to clatter. He again smiled to himself as he studied the image in his rear-view mirror and barely made out the INS car lagging behind him through the dust he kicked up. The road finally smoothed and straightened out as it curved south.

After another mile and a half, he turned back to the right. A sign marking the Spiegler Dairy sat in front of two rows of Norway Spruce evergreen trees, serving as a windbreak on the west side of the house and barn. The sheriff pulled into the broad circular barnyard in front of the sign. The now not-so-shiny fed car trailed him. Both stopped in front of the weathered cabin between the barn and the main house. Sheriff Haley turned off his engine, relieved that the beat-up pickup truck with Oklahoma plates was nowhere to be seen.

Greg Spiegler came out the back of the main house, sat down on the steps leading into the covered back porch, slid on his scuffed up barn boots, and barked across the yard, "Hey, Haley! What the hell brings you out here?"

The sheriff responded as Greg came walking over. "Hi, Greg. I have a pair of Feds here. There's a concern you might have an illegal working here on the farm."

Acting quite surprised, Greg answered, "Really?"

238

The agents introduced themselves, and Officer Stewart formally informed the farmer that the purpose for their visit comprised of investigating reported undocumented farmworkers in the area. Greg divulged to the agents he had added sixteen Holsteins to his milking stock last April and lost his hired hand. He made a call to a cousin who dairy farms in Oklahoma to see if he had an experienced farmhand he could spare for a while or knew of any dairy workers searching for work.

"Sure enough, less than three weeks later, Arturo pulled into the yard with his family. Well, son-of-a-bitch, I got a new hand. AND a good one. I paid him an honest wage like any other hand. He lived in the cabin right where you're at, and, damn, he worked hard. And Rosie, his wife, worked just as hard. It never occurred to me they coulda been wetbacks. Hell, I doubt it. No idea where they are right now, though. Probably back in Oklahoma. I do know he didn't give a damn for our winters. Arturo hated the snow."

The lower-ranking agent walked over and took a glimpse inside the cabin through the door window. He turned to Agent Stewart and shook his head no.

Just as Agent Booth began to grill Greg about when Arturo left, Charlie came walking out of the barn. Greg's attention transferred to Charlie, and he did not answer the agent. "Did you get the damn calving pen moved out of the mud hole?"

"I'll do it tomorrow."

"I told you to do it yesterday."

Charlie began to fire back, but he chose to shut up and rolled his eyes when he realized strangers were present.

Greg turned to the officers, "Arturo would never argue with me. Now I get this!" Pointing in disgust at Charlie.

John Haley voiced a hello to Charlie, who responded, "Good to see you, Sheriff. Can you get this old bastard off my back?" Using his thumb to point back at Greg. The sheriff grinned.

Greg continued, "Sorry, that's all I know, gotta get to work, and Charlie has to run to town."

With everything going on, Charlie was late for school. The agents did not recognize the duo's badgering relationship was a playful father-son interaction.

Before the junior agent continued probing regarding Arturo's departure, Agent Stewart projected, "Nice meeting you, gentlemen," referring to Greg and Charlie. He turned to the sheriff. "John, if he ever shows up around here again, call us."

Sheriff Haley presumed the senior agent intentionally cut off his partner's questions because there was no use in pressing the subject as long as the Rodriguez family had moved on. The INS agents had a full schedule for the day. The sheriff and the senior agent knew Arturo would never show up in Cresco again.

"No problem, Carl. Can you guys find your way back to town okay? I'm going the opposite way." The agents nodded, thanked the sheriff for his help, and headed to their dirty blue car. The sheriff, tempted to finger 'wash me' in the yellowish dust now caked on their trunk, watched Agent Booth jump into the driver's seat. Agent Stewart gave the remaining threesome a polite wave before he climbed in the passage door. The INS agents headed back to town the same way they came.

"You did the right thing, John, thank you."

The sheriff didn't acknowledge Greg's statement but walked over to the cabin and gazed in the window. "Looks pretty clean in there." Half laughing to himself, " Wish I could say the same for their car." He turned towards Charlie, "Hey, I remember seeing an old fishing pole leaning against the wall here last week when I stopped by." He pointed towards a spot on the cabin porch next to the door. "Yours, Charlie?"

"Naw, Coach dropped it off for Jose."

"It doesn't surprise me. Quite the guy." The sheriff nodded his head as a positive response to the coach's deed.

"He gave me a pillow that looks like a giant rainbow trout." Charlie flashed a big grin, "So I remember all the fish I wrestled. Pretty funny!"

Charlie's dad piped in, "It's my understanding he gave it to you because you were the big fish flopping around on the mat."

241

Ignoring his father, "It's in my pickup. You gotta see it, Sheriff!" Charlie turned to head to his truck.

The sheriff snickered and voiced, "Not now. I'll see it the next time I pull you over." They chuckled. Charlie even grinned, knowing there was a good chance it would happen sooner than later. Haley went on, "Now, you need to get your butt to school, or I will have to arrest you for truancy!"

"See ya, Sheriff," Charlie said as he gave the sheriff a quick little salute.

He headed to the house as his mother came rushing out, carrying a homemade apple pie in her hands. Letting the screen door bang behind her, she addressed the sheriff across the lawn, "John, you need to take this home with you for your family."

She stopped on the sidewalk when she met her son. She stuck her cheek out towards Charlie, and he responded by giving her a little kiss. "Now get!" She sternly instructed him.

The sheriff turned around and came back towards the house. He tried to refuse the pie but did not put up much of a fight. Taking a whiff of the pie, he proclaimed, "Apple, yum. My favorite!" He thanked her, said goodbye to Greg, and headed to his patrol car with a smile.

He planned to go the other way back to town using the blacktop road just a half-mile away. He did not need to hurry as it would be a ten-minute faster trip than back-tracking the way the agents drove.

242

Getting to Cresco too quickly might result in an embarrassment for the sheriff if he ran into the INS officers accidentally.

Sheriff Haley never missed a single wrestling match this past season. With his sirens blaring, he had escorted the team van out of town on their way to the state tournament. Charlie and Jose were his favorites. More importantly, for the sheriff, Annie Spiegler made excellent pies.

He slowly completed his logbook, turned on the car engine, and took off, thinking he should wash his patrol car when he got back into Cresco.

CHAPTER 22

BIG RED

Drew Parker's alarm clock buzzed at the usual time. He turned slightly, winched a little, and slapped the top of the clock to shut it down. He hesitated for just a moment. Sleep could effortlessly overtake him if he let it, and no one would question him if he just closed his eyes. Maybe being a little scared of saying the wrong words or maybe a little scared of being reminded of the agony he felt from this news, he had no desire to see this day play out.

It was not how Drew's mother and father raised him. He heard his parents, especially his dad, say it more than he chose to remember, "It's okay to be scared, but the job has to get done."

Opening his eyes, Drew studied his two favorite NFL players' posters: Mercury Morris of the Miami Dolphins, on the wall above the foot of his bed, and Ed Podolak of the Kansas City Chiefs stapled to the adjacent wall. Completing an undefeated season, Morris helped the Dolphins win the Super Bowl. Podolak grew up in a small farming community in southwest Iowa. He became an all-purpose player for the Iowa Hawkeyes before being drafted by the Chiefs. In addition to the two individual players, the Nebraska Corn Huskers Team's poster commemorating their 40-6 victory over Notre Dame in the Orange Bowl hung on the far wall. The thought of never being able to play football again raced through his mind.

Drew was well aware of the symptoms of depression from his discussions with his doctors, and he laid his head back down on his pillow, folded his hands on his chest, and silently said a little prayer asking God for courage. He was scared. Going to school and facing all the questions would be his responsibility, his job today, and the job will get done. He missed his father.

Unable to simply hop out of bed, Drew developed a new procedure. Scooting his rear end to the edge of the bed, Drew threw his legs out. He pushed himself up with his right hand rolling up like a log to a sitting position. Drew took a pair of deep breaths and rolled his neck around to get the kinks out of it. He gazed at the black sling keeping his left arm in place to protect his shoulder, which was still tender from the three-hour surgery over four weeks ago. The screws they used to re-attached the ligaments hopefully kept his shoulder from dislocating in the future. His broken collar bone and cracked shoulder blade should heal over time. Drew had been told by his mother how lucky he had been to have one of the top orthopedic surgeons in the country so close to Cresco, but he was not feeling it this morning.

He rocked himself to a standing position and stood in front of the mirror above his dresser. Drew turned his radio on out of habit and then immediately turned it off. The news was not going to be good news, and he did not want to go through the agony of it, but he needed to hear the words the radio sent out to the rest of Cresco. He turned the radio back on.

As he listened to an advertisement for the Hy-Vee Grocery Store, "with a helpful smile in every aisle," Drew secretly hoped he missed the sports news. Still, when the farm report came on, he recognized the radio program's order. After the soybean and corn prices, he listened for Pat's Radiator Repair's usual advertisement, followed by sports.

"...the best place in town to take a leak, Pat's Radiator! KCRE Cresco. Welcome to the sports report. This is Casey Prine with your local sporting news. Yesterday, the University of Nebraska announced it withdrew its football scholarship offer to Drew Parker of Cresco High School in Cresco. Parker, a first-team all-state defensive back for the Cresco Spartans, had been offered a full-ride scholarship to the University of Nebraska to play football for the Cornhuskers in the fall. Parker

247

suffered a devastating shoulder injury in his state championship wrestling match in February. Even after getting injured, Parker won the state title at 185-pounds and led the Cresco Spartans to the team championship."

This news announcement probably surprised most of the Cresco community, but Drew had a conversation with the Nebraska coaching staff the week before. Casey's radio voice continued, "We were able to interview Drew, and he confirmed to KCRE he had a dialogue with the University of Nebraska's athletic director. Although he has lost his athletic scholarship, the university restructured his financial aid offer to include an academic scholarship and grant package to attend the University of Nebraska. The Nebraska football program has committed to Drew to be an invited walk-on to the Cornhuskers football team in the fall. As an invited walk-on, the university will provide him the resources of the athletic department's medical training staff and full access to their weight training facility to rehabilitate his shoulder with the expectation Drew will play football the next season. We here at KCRE wish him the best."

A smile came across Drew's face as he fondly gazed at the picture, sitting on his dresser, of his father. "I'm going to Nebraska. Love you, Dad. Go Big Red!"

Drew hoped what came next would be different than what he was dreading. But that was not to be the case. The radio news report went on, "In somewhat related news, the Cresco School Board last night, in a unanimous decision, released Tom Kilmer from his high school teaching position and his wrestling coaching position effective immediately. Kilmer taught high school physical education and coached the Cresco Spartan wrestling team the last two seasons, where he guided the team to the state championship this past February. Earlier in the week, Kilmer pled guilty to aggravated assault charges in the Howard County Superior Court. Kilmer physically assaulted Ken Westby, the father of one of Kilmer's wrestlers at the time."

"In the police report from February 12th, Kilmer entered the Cresco American Legion Hall at 232 North Main Street and walked over to Westby, who was sitting at the bar. Unprovoked, he pulled Westby off a barstool, shoved him against the wall, and punched him in the face. Kilmer then threw Westby over the bar onto the floor. Kilmer vaulted over the bar and continued to pummel him. It took the bartender and other American Legion members to pull Kilmer off Westby. Westby suffered a broken nose, a broken arm, facial bruises, and three broken ribs. Kilmer will be placed on probation for one year and must pay Westby restitution for his medical bills and lost wages. Neither Westby nor Kilmer were available for comment."

Drew's heart sunk knowing how vital Tom and Lori Kilmer were to him. He bit his lip, shut the radio off, and, out of habit, he reached up and separated some aluminum window blind slats so he could see outside to check the weather.

The front of his car caught his attention, and he pulled the drawstrings raising the blinds to take a closer look. Someone, and he knew who, had cut out a large capital letter "N" out of red construction paper and taped it to the front of his car grill. Even from across the yard, Drew gazed at the distinctive white coffee cup with a fish handle, strategically positioned as if it were the hood ornament. It made him smile as he whispered to himself, "Well, son of a gun, he still thinks he can make me a fisherman."

The telephone rang down the hall in their family room. Drew heard his mother say hello. "Drew, it's for you!" she hollered down the hallway as she covered the receiver end of the telephone. "It's Krissy Kinsley."

"I'm coming."

As he entered the family room, his mother had returned to the telephone conversation, but Drew could not make out what she was saying. Karla turned and seeing her son, "Here's Drew. Nice talking with you, Krissy. Bye now."

Smiling at Drew, she reached out with the telephone handset and handed it to him. Grabbing the black handset with the hand of his good arm, he held it up to his ear and mouth.

Awkwardly he said, "Hello," more like a question than a statement.

"Hi Drew, it's Kris."

"Yeah, I know."

"Listen, I thought you could use a friend today with all that's going on. Maybe I can drive you to school and save your mom a trip," struggling to keep her voice chipper. Krissy recognized Drew's hesitation. "Drew, we dated for nearly three years. We were very close, but when..." she paused.

Drew finished her sentence, "when my dad died."

"Yeah, when we lost your dad, you shut me out. I knew it was important for you and your mom to figure your next steps out. But, gosh, it's been over a year. You buried yourself in football and wrestling. Then Bingo happened, your shoulder, now Nebraska, and I don't think you've had a date since then. Certainly not with me."

"You're right, Kris. I'm sorry. Jeez, has it been a year? I hadn't thought about it." He stopped and then shyly repeated, "Sorry."

"We hardly talk. I try at school, but you don't respond. We don't have to be boyfriend-girlfriend, but I don't want to lose you as a friend. Can we at least be friends?"

Again Drew hesitated and finally replied with a whisper, "I miss you." He heard her whimpering on the other end of the line, and he said, "I don't want to lose you either, but I don't think we can just be friends."

Through her sniffles, "what do you mean?"

"Well, we'll take it slow, but you missed going to Prom last year because of me."

Krissy cheered up, "So, Drew Parker, are you asking me to Prom?"

"Unless...unless you already have a date...umm, do you?"

With a slight giggle, she replied, "As a matter of fact, I do."

"Oh...," Drew felt embarrassed and shot down.

"But I think my dad would greatly appreciate NOT taking me to Prom!" It felt good for both of them to laugh together again. "I'll be there in a half-hour to pick you up."

"Hey, Krissy, do you remember our first date?"

"Oh, yeah, how could I forget. That's if you can call it a date. We were freshmen, and we decided to meet at the front gate of the high school football game. It had been raining, but it stopped before my dad dropped me off. You looked so cute standing under the little awning of the ticket booth waiting for me and trying to stay dry. You had on a hooded blue Cresco Football sweatshirt, blue Levi's, and cowboy boots."

"You remember what I was wearing? Jeez, Krissy, all I remember is walking up to the field on that thick mud-covered path and your shoe getting stuck in the mud. You pulled your foot out of your shoe, and then you were hopping around on one leg. I was helping you balance while trying to reach down in the mud to retrieve your shoe for you."

Krissy continued for him, "yup, that's when you slipped and fell into the mud and pulled me down with you."

"I still don't think so," Drew chuckled. "I reached down, and the next thing I knew, you fell into me!" They both chuckled now at the vision the memory brought. "I somehow ended up on my hands and knees in the mud, and you're sitting on me like you were getting a pony ride!"

She could feel his smile through the phone. "At least you got my shoe!... Gosh, Drew, it's sure good to hear you laugh. See you in a few."

"I can't wait to show you my car's new hood ornament. You're goin' love it...and...." In a soft, warm tone, he added, "Thanks, Krissy."

CHAPTER 23

KILMERS

Across town, Tom Kilmer turned the key and locked the front door. Pausing a second, he ran his hand across the rounded face of the solid walnut door, knowing how much his wife loved its shape. Though he never confessed it to her, he loved it, too. Tom closed the storm door behind him. With a clang, he threw the house keys into the metal mailbox on the brick wall. He closed the mailbox lid, stepped back, and examined the house for one last time. Lori came up from behind, laid her head between his shoulder blades, and hugged him around his chest. Coach let her stay for a moment. He felt her warmth, her love, and her compassion which comforted him. He loved her so much that he contemplated asking her if he had told her lately that he loved her. But not being in a playful mood, Tom let the moment slide.

The public façade identified Tom as the man of the house, the fit, and the strong athlete. But the wrestling coach knew the strength of their marriage

255

belonged to his beautiful spouse. She provided the dreams, the courage, the drive, and the inspiration. Tom believed he let her down. His eyes began to water up. He had no desire to move as he sensed her love coming through her embrace. He turned his shoulders to reach back with one arm, like a wrestling "Whizzer," around her head, shifting her to his side, hugging her neck. She kept her arms around him.

They scanned the house simultaneously one last time. It was the home they planned to purchase and where they would raise a family. Tom kissed his wife on the forehead. They did not say it aloud, but they both knew they were lucky their landlord disagreed with the school board's ruling. He thought Ken Westby got what he deserved, and he had no issues with letting the pair out of their lease. The Kilmers appreciated him for the opportunity for a quick clean getaway to begin a new life away from Cresco.

Coach took a deep breath and sighed, not intentionally meaning it to be a cue, but both recognized it was time to leave. She let go, and they turned and strolled hand in hand towards the green mist Chevy Nova, loaded full to the back window. They packed all week after the school superintendent put Tom on leave until the school board met the evening before releasing him officially. He closed the U-Haul trailer door, maneuvered the complicated latch, and fastened the Masterlock padlock to secure it. Lori climbed into the passenger side as Coach 'double-checked' the trailer hitch for the sixth or seventh time. Tom climbed in behind the wheel and started the engine. Before putting it in gear, he turned to his partner. "I have one stop before we leave town."

"I know," She answered.

They turned down Elm Street and headed east to the edge of town. Tom slowed the car and took a right turn through a narrow gate onto a limestone gravel driveway. Vigilantly watching the U-Haul trailer in his side mirror, Tom made sure he did not cut the corner too tight. Maneuvering the road up to the point where it looped back around, Tom circled and faced the car and trailer back towards the road. He put the car in park and turned off the ignition. Neither one had spoken a word since leaving the house. Coach started to open his car door, and his mate did the same. He stopped and reached across the car seat, and put his hand on her leg. Lori instantly realized Tom intended to do this by himself. She gave him a tight-lipped smile of understanding, quietly pulled her car door back, and closed it. Tears built in his eyes, but he abruptly turned away and exited the car. He gently closed the door as if he meant not to disturb her or maybe to prolong his mission.

Lori watched him walk across the grass, but when tears blurred her vision, she turned the other way, not wanting him to see her sobbing. Waiting felt painful as she kept trying to hold back her tears. She clutched a Kleenex and tried to take deep breaths through her nose while exhaling out through her mouth. The minutes seemed like hours, and sniffles kept coming.

She heard the soft steps in the grass being replaced by the crunch of the gravel. Lori continued to stare the other way as she dabbed her eyes, hoping he would not recognize that she had been crying. She heard him open the door and plop into the driver's seat with a sigh. The car door closed behind him. She turned to see Tom put the key in the ignition, but he did not turn it over. Tom put both hands on the steering wheel and stared out the windshield. Lori noticed his chest starting to heave as he took bigger and deeper breaths, and he finally stammered, "I love you."

Unable to stop the tears now, they gushed down her face. She reached for Tom only to see his tears streaming down. They reacted to each other by sliding across the bench seat, meeting in the middle. They hung onto each other like high school sweethearts as if they were telling each other never to let go. Their tears turned to sobs. They were finally able to speak when the weeping waned, saying "I love you" back and forth repeatedly.

Lori finally muttered. "It's going to be all right."

"Ya, sure, you betcha!" Tom spit out.

They both laughed as they regained their

composure. Lori directed him not to use his sleeve to wipe his nose. Tom snorted as he accepted her offer of a tissue causing Lori to giggle when she handed him a Kleenex. They each dabbed their eyes. Tom wiped his nose, then he cocked his head to the side, grinned at his spouse, and softly declared, "You know, Honey, these kids have been our family 'til now, but I think it's time for us to have our own children. What do you think?"

Lori squeezed her husband's hand. "I think it's a pretty good idea, Sweetie, because...because I'm pregnant."

It took a moment for the news to sink in on Tom, "You're having a baby?"

His wife nodded as she picked up his hand and kissed the back of it and, sarcastically, whispered in his ear, "I think that's what being pregnant means," and kissed his cheek. "Get it?"

"Well, I'll be damned. Got it." He slid back over in front of the steering wheel, started the car, placed it into gear.

As he gradually took his foot off the break, they heard the tires on the gravel as they slowly rolled down the lane. Lori spotted the broad smile growing on her husband's face, causing her to beam. Stopping the car one more time at the gate, Tom gazed back over his left shoulder. He clearly viewed, draped over the top of the stone cross rising above the polished granite headstone, the floppy brown fishing hat with fishing flies hooked in the mesh band. "If it's a boy, I know what we will name him."

He read aloud the words engraved in the headstone. "Rest in Peace, William 'Bing' Natvig, STATE CHAMPION." Tom's shimmering gold medallion dangled down by its lanyard from the horizontal bar of the cross. Swaying with his medallion were seven other glistening gold medals.

ABOUT THE AUTHOR

Dale Stopperan lives in Spokane, Washington but grew up in the rural community of Cresco, Iowa. His high school coaches were instrumental role models in Mr. Stopperan becoming a teacher, coach, and principal working in the public school system for thirty seven years. His experience as a middle school and high school wrestling coach provided a basis for the novel "Wrestling with Tradition."

Made in United States
Orlando, FL
20 September 2022

22622353R00143